# The Continuing Professional Development of Educators: emerging European issues

Edited by
**ALEX ALEXANDROU,
KIT FIELD & HELEN MITCHELL**

SYMPOSIUM
BOOKS

**Symposium Books**
PO Box 204, Didcot, Oxford OX11 9ZQ, United Kingdom
*the book publishing division of wwwords Ltd*
www.symposium-books.co.uk


Published in the United Kingdom, 2005


ISBN 1 873927 25 8

Typeset by wwwords Ltd
Printed and bound in the United Kingdom by Cambridge University Press

# Contents

# Preface

As a concept, continuing professional development (CPD) continues to grow in importance within a European context, with both the European Union and its constituent governments placing a great emphasis on lifelong learning and on educators improving their performance, becoming more efficient and effective and delivering a better service.

To this end the International Professional Development Association (IPDA) has, over more than three decades, sought to support, develop and promote good professional practice by providing forums and promoting networks for individuals concerned with professional development, gathering and disseminating information, monitoring and evaluating policy and practice developments and giving advice on the development of policy and practice.

However, the IPDA felt that more could be done and to this end has tasked us with producing this book, which seeks to go beyond merely criticising what has happened to date. Our aim is to take a critical look at CPD policy and practice from a broad European perspective, examining both values and paradigms. In turn it is hoped this will highlight models and concepts and how these relate to cultural contexts, which will develop lessons to be learnt.

Writers have been commissioned from across professions and from several European countries to attack this issue. Not only has a generic European perspective been put forward but so have perspectives from both northern and southern Europe with a touch of North America to add a little spice. This is an eclectic mix of views and standpoints which are inextricably linked by the editors' and authors' profound belief that only through CPD can progress be achieved at both an individual and an organisational level.

We hope our book will provide some answers, be informative, stimulate positive debate among both academics and practitioners and, as always, encourage others to research and publish in this area.

**Alex Alexandrou, Kit Field & Helen Mitchell**

CHAPTER 1

---

# Continuing Professional Development and Networking in Europe

## MAGNUS PERSSON

### From Comenius to Comenius

Four hundred years ago, in seventeenth-century Europe, medieval scholars kept a firm hold on the curriculum and teaching. For the few students allowed to attend education all teaching was in Latin. The norm was lifeless learning by rote under the stroke of the whip. Teaching was mechanically drummed into the pupils. It was empty and dry, segregated from real life and knowledge.

At that time a man by the name of Jan Amos Komensky entered the scene, describing the prevailing system as 'a torture chamber for brains'. Step by step he formulated a new view on knowledge and learning, on the school system and on didactics. This man was later forever to be remembered in European educational history under his Latin name, Johann Amos Comenius. He was a thinker on didactics and pedagogy who would strongly contribute to reforming the concepts of education.

Comenius was the very first person to advocate education for everyone in the true sense. It was based on humanism, broad-based knowledge and an orientation towards 'the things themselves' – adapted to children's conceptions and their needs. He argued that the aim of education was to get free of prejudice and idols, in order to find the truth behind these. We should all strive to cultivate mankind, and in education cautiously maintain and watch over the pupil during a slowly progressing and developing process. Teaching should be a reflection of life, related to the environment formed by people and the surrounding world. Throughout his life, Johann Amos Comenius worked for educational, scientific and cultural cooperation, enlightenment and understanding, social peace and the unity of mankind. Do not these statements strike a chord of recognition in us all?

The school of developing of knowledge advocates reason and optimism, that a person is good by nature and that people can change, and believes in progression in learning. I believe we can embrace this and follow the historical path from Socrates and Comenius to Rousseau and Marx, Piaget and Vygotsky and the twentieth-century reform pedagogues.

Moving 350 years forward in time, to the 1990s, many of us are closely linked with Comenius again, by networking within the European Union's (EU's) Socrates and Leonardo educational programmes, and within the Comenius action. The European scenario, including education, has been suddenly changing, bringing discussion on all levels from EU policy making to classroom performance. So, then, what has been on the agenda for education during the last 10 years?

### The European Agenda

In the mid 1990s, among the many complex changes taking place in European society, three major trends were particularly manifest. The first was the impact of the information society, not only transforming the nature of work and the organisation of production but also strongly influencing the methods and strategies for teaching and learning. The second was the impact of internationalisation, not only radically affecting trade, removing the barriers between labour markets, but also quite suddenly making schools and educational organisations realise the need to take on an international perspective. The third was the impact of the scientific and technical world, which led not only to the emergence of more sophisticated products and new production methods, but also 'overnight' to the provision of computers, e-mail, the Internet, mobile phones and a plethora of new technological words for teachers and students.

The European Commission's answer – and proposed solution – to these challenges came in 1995 in a White Paper titled *Teaching and Learning: towards the learning society* (European Commission, 1995), focusing on broad-based knowledge and employability. This was followed by an additional policy document, *Towards a Knowledge of Europe* (European Commission, 1997). The learning society was and is facing a double challenge, both to take better care of and strengthen the main resource, which is the human resource, and to combat social exclusion in order to reduce the risk of social gaps dramatically occurring in society. In a society in which everyone is obliged to understand complex situations which fluctuate unpredictably and where one is swamped by a vast quantity of varied information, there is an apparent risk of a rift between those who are able to interpret, those who can only use and those who can do neither.

From this EU initiative all of us saw ourselves in a growing debate about quality and efficiency in school education, and on strengthening language learning, and attempts were made to enhance flexibility and mobility in systems and in work.

Following the White Paper, 1996 was proclaimed the Year of Lifelong Learning. At the same time the Commission took another initiative called 'Learning in the Information Society' in an initial effort to define objectives and priorities for European schools' entry into the information society. One purpose was to encourage the educational use of multimedia and to create a 'critical mass' of users, products and educational services. Another reason was to strengthen the European dimension in culture and language in education with the help of information and communication technology (ICT).

In 1997 the concept of the new, second-generation Socrates programme for education was introduced, aiming for 'the gradual construction of an open and dynamic European educational area' and formally launched in 2000. The three objectives for the present Socrates programme are: (1) increasing the access of European citizens to the full range of Europe's education resources; (2) innovation in resources; and (3) wide dissemination of good practice in education. It might be interesting to know that this was also the starting point of Comenius 3 networks from 2001, in line with the new objectives.

One basic starting point has to be stressed. Whenever we talk about Europe and education and training we need to bear in mind that all decisions on education have to be taken on national, regional and local levels, closely connected to linguistic, cultural and social factors. The EU is not allowed to intervene either in the national organisation of education or in the forming of educational content. The Community is furthermore not supposed to harmonise legislation etceteras on a European level. This is clearly stated in Article 149 of the EU Treaty.

In March 2000 the leaders of the EU member states met in Lisbon, agreeing on common objectives and forming and adapting a text into the Lisbon Declaration on education and training. The EU is not looking for a US model, but instead developing a social model where human resources are one of the main tools. The strategic goal for the EU to 2010 defines Europe as becoming the most competitive and dynamic knowledge-based economy in the world, capable of sustainable economic growth with more and better jobs, and greater social cohesion. The so-called Lisbon strategy indicated dense cooperation and phased objectives of education and training systems in Europe, which were followed by an extensive discussion in Copenhagen on vocational education. The process of coordination within higher education, for example regarding diplomas, was initiated in Bologna, followed by coordination on context. At a summit in 2002 a European lifelong learning strategy was adopted.

The EU works with systems which are included in the so-called 'open method of cooperation': common objectives, indicators and benchmarks, the exchange of good practice and peer reviews. The recently adapted work programme for cooperation consists of three strategic objectives, 13 objectives and 33 indicative indicators.

Europe is facing major challenges within education when looking some years ahead. In Europe about 1.4 million teachers will retire before 2010, resulting in a drain of professional experience and a substantially lowered average age of teachers in Europe and of course showing a massive need for recruiting new teachers. At the same time education is undergoing rapid change due to new technology, new learning approaches and research and an expectation of education that differs from before. Which are the skills necessary to have for the future in order to be active citizens and for working in the future labour market? The answer to this question emphasises the necessity of finding sustainable conceptual frameworks for learning in the twenty-first century, thereby also addressing the thematic area of the Learning Teacher Network, being the new role of the teacher.

In 2003 the European Council defined five reference levels of European average performance in education and training: in other words five benchmarks. These are related to the three strategic objectives of the detailed work programme for cooperation.

The first strategic objective targets the improvement of quality and effectiveness of education and training systems in the EU. The objectives under this heading address the development of skills essential for the knowledge society, increased recruitment to scientific and technical studies, ensured access to ICT for everyone and making the best use of resources.

Two benchmarks are tied to this strategic objective.

- *Basic skills.* By 2010, the percentage of low-achieving 15-year-olds in reading literacy in the EU should have decreased by at least 20% compared to 2000, which means a reduction from 17.2% of the pupils to under 14%.
- *Mathematics, science and technology.* The total number of graduates in mathematics, science and technology in the EU should increase by at least 15% by 2010 while at the same time the level of gender imbalance should decrease.

Regarding investment in education and training, a Lisbon objective states the ambition of 'a substantial yearly increase in investment in human resources'.

The second strategic objective recognises the importance of facilitating the access of all to education and training systems, by making learning more attractive, creating open learning environments and supporting active citizenship, equal opportunities and social cohesion.

Again, two benchmarks are related to this strategic objective.

- *Early school leavers.* By 2010, an EU average-rate European benchmark of no more than 10% early school leavers should be achieved.
- *Completion of upper secondary school.* By 2010, at least 85% of 22-year-olds in the EU should have completed upper secondary education.

Examining the third strategic objective we find a determination to open up education and training systems to the wider world. This openness is to be associated with the issue of connecting education and training to working life and research, and the growth of a spirit of enterprise. Furthermore, it emphasises the learning of foreign languages, the importance of mobility and exchange and the efforts to be made in strengthening European cooperation. It goes without saying that these last points correlate very well with the topic of international networking.

These objectives are all addressing one of the key expressions of European education and networking today: the concept of lifelong learning. The fifth benchmark refers to this.

- The average EU level of participation in lifelong learning should be at least 12.5% of the adult working age population; today the number is only 8.5%. The definition here is the percentage of the population participating in education and training in the four weeks prior to the survey.

In all five benchmarks, these aims reflect high ambition and a substantial improvement compared with the present situation.

### Lifelong and Life-wide Learning

Let us pay some attention to the issue of lifelong learning, which is not the same as continuing education in the formal education system. On the contrary, lifelong learning crosses over or 'dissolves' boundaries, regardless of observing subjects and courses or policy sectors. Lifelong learning is a holistic view of education and recognises learning from a number of different environments. The concept consists of two dimensions. The lifelong dimension indicates that the individual learns throughout his/her life span. The life-wide dimension recognises formal, non-formal and informal learning. Lifelong learning and life-wide learning are issues for educational policy, labour market policy and the workplace as well as civil society.

The concept of lifelong learning is not new, but its importance has varied over time and place. The form remains, but the contents vary, which is worth bearing in mind when comparing earlier and current debate on lifelong learning. This in itself is not remarkable: political ideas and concepts may re-emerge with different attributions depending on interests and context. There are a number of words with undoubted political and rhetorical power which function as 'semantic magnets' and which are given an interpretation to serve different interests. Democracy, justice and freedom are some; lifelong learning is another. These terms in themselves are ambiguous (Skolverket, 2000).

The idea of lifelong learning was first introduced 30 years ago by UNESCO and – together with closely related ideas on *éducation permanente* from the Council of Europe – immediately made a great impact in the debate on educational policy. Then, as now, the debate centred also on the individual's responsibility for taking advantage of the opportunities provided by lifelong learning. Lifelong learning should be understood against the background of the political cultures of the times. The idea was grounded in a humanistic tradition and interwoven with expectations of self-realisation, equality, a better society and a higher quality of life. However, being too vague, these ideas were not transformed into implementable strategies.

At the end of the 1980s and throughout the whole of the 1990s, the idea of lifelong learning resurfaced but in a different policy context. As described earlier, throughout Europe, and as formulated in EU policies but also by the Organisation for Economic Cooperation and Development in 1996, lifelong learning was now used in a more narrow interpretation responding to the needs of the economy for skilled labour with the necessary competence.

Where does this leave us? Well, we would conclude that the individual's learning is to be regarded as a lifelong project, which takes place not only in formal educational contexts, but also in all human activity. People learn throughout their lives, from the cradle to the grave (which we call lifelong learning), and they learn from all aspects of life (which is defined as life-wide learning). This requires a new educational perspective. At the same time lifelong learning can neither be implemented from above nor be controlled. The starting point must be the individual and an appreciation that different people have different needs which vary over time. At each moment of time in an individual's life span, there should be appropriate educational opportunities with the requirement also of being equally distributed.

Living in the information society creates a demand for flexibility and open-minded approaches to solutions, hence forcing education to provide for elements of lifelong skills. If teachers and trainers are to prepare an even more diverse group of pupils and students for much more challenging work – for framing problems; investigating, integrating and synthesising information; creating new solutions; learning on their own; and working cooperatively – they will need substantially more and new knowledge, and radically different skills than most now have.

Taking the individual perspective leads to demands for study guidance and counselling, individual study plans and a variety of educational environments which can satisfy the needs and backgrounds of people. Personalised learning would be the educational focus, thus also implicitly announcing the arrival of flexible learning, independent of location, specific institutions and time of day. Therefore, the concept of e-learning is closely connected. In practice this also means that the view of knowledge, what the school should teach, is shifted from specific subjects to the individual's learning potential. Explicitly, the individual is clearly the sole owner of his or her own knowledge. As a consequence, we need to raise the issue of *which* knowledge and competence is to be predominant for the future.

### Professional Learning Communities

This macro context gives the need to address key issues vital to education. Are schools prepared for the future, or do we believe that the *status quo* will do? Learning is taking place everywhere and all the time; is there learning only schools can provide, or could learners get education for life anywhere else? Do schools give learners the power of and responsibility for their own learning and, if so, to what extent? When asking teachers about who is responsible for the school, why do they answer 'the headteacher'? When asking students about who is responsible for their learning, why do they answer 'the teacher'? Are schools framing questions for thinking, reflection and learning, or are the learners simply responding to curriculum requirements and facts from textbooks? What constitutes and promotes good learning? Are schools today actually learning communities in a true sense?

The well-known researcher Michael Fullan makes the point that research on educational change is a young branch of science, finding the lack of systematised study of educational change remarkable (Fullan, 1991). Not until the 1960s did we start to understand how school improvement works in practice. He describes four phases of development since that time, where the 1980s and 1990s showed what he calls *intensification* by accentuation of the 'what' and 'how' in teaching, and *restructuring* by school-based autonomy in starting to create responsibilities, common objectives, cultures of cooperation and radical transformation of teacher training.

However, more recently Fullan (2001) has argued that there is a recent remarkable convergence of theories, knowledge bases, ideas and strategies that help us confront complex problems that do not have easy answers. This convergence creates a new mind-set – a framework for thinking about and leading complex change. He summarises that there seem to be five components of leadership that represent independent but mutually reinforcing forces for positive change. These are as follows.

- The first is *moral purpose*, which means acting with the intention of making a positive difference in the lives of employees, customers and society as a whole.
- The second is *understanding the change process*, where he claims that moral purpose must be interlinked with a healthy respect for the complexities of the change process, in order to be successful.
- The third is that *relationships improve,* which is found to be the single factor common to every successful change initiative.
- The fourth is *creating and sharing knowledge*, where the new work in this area shows a congruence with the previous three themes and reveals that new theoretical and empirical studies of successful organisations unpack the operational meaning of the general term 'knowledge organisation'.
- The fifth is *coherence making*, as all this complexity keeps people on the edge of chaos: balancing enough ambiguity to keep creativity flowing but along the way – and when sufficient – a group seeks and needs coherence.

What is increasingly clear is the need to create professional learning communities, in schools, within organisations and in networks. In schools it is essential to manage and develop human resources and give the investment in people the priority it deserves. The complexity of teaching and learning today makes it impossible to remain as a single performing teacher, closed from the surrounding world and from colleagues. More and more important for success and for reaching objectives are to work together, interact and communicate with others, not only to gain professionally but also to empower others and to develop professional connections. Dialogue and communication are fundamental and it is more than a way of finding solutions to problems. Dialogue means to start from an attitude where the objective truth does not exist, but instead different truths depending on the choice of perspective. To describe a landscape round a house gives different answers depending which window you are looking from. In order to deepen the understanding of other people's thoughts and ideas – and to find understanding and acceptance of each other – people need to move to each other's windows. To take time to understand someone else's perspective means a challenge to your own conceptions and dealing with your own learning. Divergent views on the issue are vital, and show in the interaction between people. A continuing dialogue instead of a rigid standpoint, an open mind instead of a closed mind, motivation and curiosity instead of resignation, are tools for lifelong learning instead of daily tests. This is the challenge of interactive professionalism.

By doing so, the aim would be to build a common vision for learning and doing, describing where to go, why and how, and from there creating the future as a community of learners, where teachers as well as students learn as learners and together with each other. By doing so, there is also a platform to combat alienation, which is a growing problem, and to provide to all professionals and learners a learning and social community that is inclusive and distributed. The essential issue for everyone of how to be motivated and valued goes hand in hand with the concept of a learning community.

There is to be seen a changing discourse from management to leadership to leadership for learning. For headteachers, this means a change from planning and organising the content of teachers' workload to leading their learning. By this it is understood that the headteacher needs to contribute to a deepened understanding of the mission as well as creating meetings where teachers' notions of teaching in relation to pupils' learning are challenged.

Another characteristic of a learning community is to develop a professional culture and knowledge base, by researching, sharing and improving educational practice to improve learners' learning. As a professional it is essential to keep learning at the centre of all activities, and to learn with the learners. Learning is a doing word, as Harris & Lambert (2003, p. xvi) put it – it only exists through its manifestations and it is profoundly interpersonal. All learning as well as social and intellectual growth occurs in the meeting between people, where teacher leadership and two-way communication are crucial.

A university study conducted in Karlstad in 2003 (Groth, 2004) sums up that the most important task for the teacher is to lead the pupil's learning processes. The most important task for the headteacher is to support and challenge the teacher's learning processes, and the most important task for the location's education authority is to lead the headteacher's learning processes.

The importance of reflection as a basic part of professional life is to be stressed. Lack of time is one of the factors that most strongly brings superficial solutions. The compression of time and space has real advantages, for example the pace of turnover increases, travel is faster, decisions can be taken more quickly, the level of service rises and there is less waiting time. However, the compression of time and space has its price in the function of learning, in the quality of our private and professional lives, as well as impacting on the ethics of our actions. In a learning environment there has to be defined time for reflection with regard to both working and processes. Imagine learners spending a 45-minute lesson just working and processing a product and then proceeding on to another similar lesson, and so on, without time allocated for reflection on what took place, on the results and on what you *de facto* have learnt. Without time for reflection the process is merely an act of pure consumption, not of true reasoning, conclusion drawing and learning. Reflecting on learning and experiences leads to new reflections, thus being a base for continuous learning and doing. The focus must be on the process through which learning takes place.

In a professional learning community learners ask questions such as 'What are schools for?', 'What happened during this session?', 'How do learners learn the best?', 'How can I improve in supporting the learner?', 'How do we know that this is true?' and 'Why did this work out so well this time?' Asking questions and reflecting on the answers is vital for learning, for improving and for the creation of new knowledge. Learning is not only about information: it is about problem solving, adapting, adjusting, transferring and transforming, thus creating continuous learning. A professional teacher working for 25 years may have one year of experience 25 times, but preferably the case is 25 years of experience by developing as a learner him- or herself. By evolving strategies for learning, strategies for values and conscious approaches we give a true contribution to a learner's lifelong growth from a beginner to a master.

Follow-up and evaluation are also matters of great importance. In order to build knowledge about learning and teaching it is essential that the professionals get a response from the surrounding world. The focus for evaluation needs to be on the process between goals and results (Utbildningsdepartementet, 2001).

Learning is closely related to understanding and therefore one benchmark is the emphasis on *learning with understanding*. Often learners have limited opportunities to understand or make sense of topics because many curricula or teachers have emphasised memory rather than understanding. Textbooks are filled with facts that learners are supposed to memorise, and most tests assess learners' abilities to remember the facts. The information society showers us all with facts and information from early morning to late evening. Simply by surfing the Internet you can obtain more written facts than ever were available throughout history. Factual knowledge is of course important for thinking and problem solving. However, education today needs to help learners to sort and handle all this information, to create a meaning and structure and to be a venue for critical thinking and for face-to-face and group discussions on how to relate to and exist in this new environment. Research shows clearly that 'usable knowledge' is not the same as a mere list of disconnected facts. What characterises the professional's or expert's knowledge is that it is connected and organised around important concepts, for example the concept of tolerance (Bradford et al, 2003). Knowledge is a question of context, to understand something and be able to transfer this knowledge to other contexts and use it in other situations. As Nobel laureate Herbert Simon (1996) stated, the meaning of 'knowing' has shifted from being able to remember and repeat information to being able to find and use it.

Understanding may mean different things. One may have *understanding of* the complexity of being a teacher or a headteacher. On the other hand, one may have *the ability to understand* and grasp intellectual thoughts, concepts or context, or theory. The ability to understand is a key factor for continuous learning within and about daily practice.

An emphasis on understanding leads to a focus on *the processes of knowing*, a field of research connected to, for example, Piaget and Vygotsky. Everyone has learning competencies – understanding, resources and interests – on which to build. Humans come to formal education with a range of prior knowledge, skills, beliefs and concepts that influence what they notice about the environment and how they organise and interpret it. People construct new knowledge based on their current knowledge. Learning does not begin from knowing nothing to learning that is based on entirely new information.

Since understanding is viewed as important, people must learn to recognise when they understand and when they need more information. Therefore, it is to be viewed as important to help learners take control of their own learning. What strategies might they use to assess whether they understand someone else's meaning? Teachers have a critical role in mentoring learners to engage their understanding, building on learners' understanding, correcting misconceptions and observing and engaging with learners during the processes of learning. The most effective learning occurs when learners apply what they have learned to various and diverse new situations. An individual moves from being a novice in a subject area towards developing competency in that area through a series of learning processes. For learners and learning this is a matter of developing expertise and competent performance.

## European Networking

Research conducted by the US sociologist Ronald Inglehart proves a change of values in society that he calls *The Silent Revolution* (Inglehart, 1977). Silently and slowly Western society has transformed from a focus on material welfare and physical security towards the emphasising of quality of life in a wide sense – post-materialistic values. Our challenges for tomorrow lie in the fact that values change, that technology revolutionises the way we communicate, not only ourselves but also our thoughts and our learning. The trend from unity to diversity, from parochial values to global thinking, from immobility to mobility – of course all these shifts in the minds of young people have a major impact on how education is to develop. Only 10-15 years ahead the teenagers of today will be the decision makers, and their values will be paramount.

The rationale of the Learning Teacher Network is a number of coinciding shifts of paradigm deriving from the information- and knowledge-based society, such as:

- a transition from teaching to learning, and the creation of professional learning communities;
- a transition from factual knowledge to advanced knowledge and understanding of context;
- teachers, leaders and trainers must themselves be in the process of continuous learning;
- difficulties in recruiting teachers and leaders, which has to be met by making explicit future competences and requirements.

These shifts of paradigm are creating major challenges to the educational community in all parts of Europe. The answers have to be framed by the professionals themselves but through conscious and extended cooperation with research and researchers. For sure we know that change is the only certainty. But change is not revolution; change happens through a series of small steps. Change can only be realised by a focus on schools as professional learning communities, and school development and successful strategies growing from a bottom-up perspective. Hence, we strongly advocate the power of the professionals, aiming to enhance professional empowerment. Teacher empowerment and school development are still to be bedfellows.

The development of professional learning communities is crucial to education, but is also a basic approach to our networking (Persson, 2004). Summarised, a learning community could be based on four distinguishing features, always to be related to the increasing importance of sustainability:

- *continuous learning*, as professionals need to be skilled in the identification and understanding of learners' learning processes, not only the learners but then also one's own, in the context of continuous learning; and it is required that he or she allocates time for observation and tries to find evidence, asking 'Why?' and 'What practice makes a difference?';
- *interaction and communication*, as practitioners must have the ability to communicate around aspects of learning and, by doing this, interact with learners and professional colleagues; and in this also developing skills for coaching and mentoring;
- *ownership and management of change*, as professionals are to be the actual change agents, owning the processes and being equipped with consciousness, flexibility and skills to manage change and adjust practice from a learning perspective; and integrating follow-up and evaluation;
- *reflection*, which has to be an integral part of education for today and tomorrow.

Writing in *Creating the Future School*, Beare (2001, p. 185) concluded with these words about those who will work in the school of the future:

> This terrain is not for the immature, the shallow, the unworthy, the unformed, or the uninformed, and society needs to be very careful about what people it commissions for this task.

* * * * *

I have made this extensive exposition of key issues not only to show the reasons why – and the context and the framework in which – education and training are functioning today, but also to pinpoint the existence and core principles of the Learning Teacher Network.

The Learning Teacher Network is an international professional learning community in itself, a European platform for professionals to discover, disclose, share experience and reflect and act upon findings. We elaborate in the thematic area on the new role of the teacher and try to derive principles from school practice, research and the sharing of knowledge. It is a professional journey, not a blind search but a quest with a direction and an aim. There are no recipes but a portfolio of choices. So, the network is also about capacity building, where we, by interacting and discussing professionally, get new knowledge and strengthen our personal and joint strategies for learning.

At the moment the network is composed of 26 partners and around 50 associated member institutions from 20 European countries, ranging from pre-schools, primary and secondary schools to universities and support organisations. Actually, in reality, the set of connections demonstrates a network of networks. It is one of rather few Comenius 3 thematic networks, funded by the European Commission, and presently the only thematic network specifically addressing the thematic area of the new role of the teacher. As a network we are aiming:

- to contribute to some answers to key questions;
- to reach a growing number of professionals and institutions, involve them in thematic discussions and by this bring added value and make a difference;
- and finally, to impact on decision makers all over Europe.

I believe that the Learning Teacher Network will make a small but focused contribution to the three levers of success expressed in the joint interim report of the European Council and the European Commission (Council of the European Union, March 2004), by addressing key areas, addressing matters within the concept of lifelong learning and through our networking and actions making a contribution to a Europe of education and training.

Educationalists, practitioners and institutions participate in the network activities to gain added value and to cooperate and interact in finding joint answers to the challenges to education, by creating and sharing knowledge. Networking is learning in itself, meeting colleagues from other cultures and school systems, and with trust giving and sharing experiences, expertise, thoughts and knowledge. Today networking is essential as a working method between schools or professionals and in regions, but cooperating in a European context with colleagues throughout the continent is even more exciting and resulting – and demanding, of course. Simultaneously the commitment from network participants is overwhelmingly strong.

I strongly believe that the fundamental values, a response to the European agenda and the educational challenges, the context of lifelong learning and professional learning communities and the benefit of addressing thematic areas through multinational discussions are strong and vital motives for thematic networking in education in Europe today. Trying to explore and establish a European conceptual framework is in line with crucial educational development in European countries, as we face the same challenges and need a wider perspective in responding to these. I also believe that networking is mainly about open-mindedness, professionalism and relationships – and if existing, good progression will be found and successful results will be shown. And, from our experience, networking is highly confidence building.

### A New Generation of European Educational Programmes

Looking ahead, the EU is launching the third generation of educational programmes for the period 2007-13. Needless to say, the overall goal for what is called Education & Training 2010 is to support the achievement of the Lisbon objectives. To be underlined, the new programmes are proposed to be much more flexible than is the case today, and a radical change of perspective is proposed, as up to 80% of all project funding might be decentralised – the reverse of the situation today.

The new generation of programmes will encompass only four parts, which means a system more focused and including fewer separate actions than at present. The major programme will be the so-called Integrated Action Programme in Lifelong Learning and will comprise four sectoral programmes: Comenius (school education), Erasmus (higher education), Leonardo da Vinci (vocational education) and Grundtvig (adult education). Even though these names might be familiar, the new programme is suggested to be substantially more integrated, connecting the sectoral programmes and offering more flexible potential within each programme.

To ensure the success of the new programme the European Commission has recommended the European Parliament to allocate an overwhelming sum for this new programme –13.6 billion Euros over seven years – which is significantly more than the present budget.

A number of quantified and ambitious targets have been defined to motivate this budget:

- at least one pupil in 20 in the EU to take part in Comenius during the period of the programme;
- by 2011 to reach the target of 3 million Erasmus students since the establishment of the programme;
- 150,000 placements in companies each year under Leonardo da Vinci in 2013;
- 25,000 adults each year benefiting from training/mobility under Grundtvig in 2013.

For anyone working within education in Europe the new programmes will provide even more interesting prospects for the future, thus opening doors for extensive networking. From a professional point of view the years to come will be exciting for everyone wishing to participate in – and to form – educational development. From another and general point of view the goals and the funding provided are all about supporting European citizenship: to create modern education for 'young and old' to outline a well-functioning society ahead and a predicted better future for all.

In this networking, facing these European challenges, we can and should all contribute.

### References

Beare, H. (2001) *Creating the Future School.* London: Falmer Press.

Bradford, J., Brown, A. & Cocking, R. (Eds) (2003) *How People Learn – brain, mind, experience and school: expanded edition,* Washington, DC: National Academy Press.

Council of the European Union (2004) *Education and Training 2010: the success of the Lisbon Strategy hinges on urgent reforms.* Joint interim report of the Council and the Commission on the implementation of the detailed work programme on the follow-up of the objectives of education and training systems in Europe. Outcome of proceedings, 3 March 2004, 6905/04.

European Commission (1995) *Teaching and Learning: towards the learning society,* MEMO/95/162.

European Commission (1997) *Towards a Europe of Knowledge,* COM(97)563 final.

Fullan, M. (1991) *The New Meaning of Educational Change.* London: Cassell.

Fullan, M. (2001) *Leading in a Culture of Change.* San Francisco: Jossey-Bass.

Groth, E. (2004) *School as a Learning Organisation – from theory to practice.* Karlstad: Karlstads universitet.

Harris, A. & Lambert, L. (2003) *Building Leadership Capacity for School Improvement*. Maidenhead: Open University Press.

Inglehart, R. (1977) *The Silent Revolution*. Princeton: Princeton University Press.

Persson, M. (Ed.) (2004) *Towards the Teacher as a Learner*. Karlstad: Knappen.

Simon, H.A. (1996) Observations on the Sciences of Science Learning, paper prepared for the Committee on Developments in the Science of Learning for the Sciences of Science Learning: an interdisciplinary discussion. Department of Psychology, Carnegie Mellon University.

Skolverket (2000) *Lifelong Learning and Lifewide Learning*. Stockholm: Skolverket.

Utbildningsdepartementet (2001) *Lärande Ledare*. Stockholm: Utbildningsdepartementets Rapport nr 4.

CHAPTER 2

# Mentor Professional Development in England

## HELEN MITCHELL

### History and Context of Initial Teacher Training

The role of school-based mentors in initial teacher training (ITT) began to develop in the late 1980s and has increased rapidly in scope and importance over the past decade. Since the Secretary of State specified criteria for ITT courses leading to Qualified Teacher Status (QTS) in 1984 (Department for Education and Science, 1984), there have been seven major revisions to the statutory regulations governing ITT programmes (circulars 24/89, 9/92, 14/93, 10/97, 4/98, 4/99 and Department for Education and Skills & Teacher Training Agency [DfES & TTA], 2002). These successive changes in policy directed at ITT resulted from parallel changes in policy directed at schools as part of the move to, in the words of the Department for Education and Employment (DfEE) (1998), 'modernise' the teaching profession and to raise achievement through increased 'teacher effectiveness'.

In a bid to 'raise standards' and address issues of recruitment and retention in teaching, teacher educators were mandated to move from largely theory-based teacher education programmes to practical problem-based programmes with a strong requirement for learning through school-based experience. In 2002, working partnerships between ITT providers and schools became a requirement included in the main body of the Qualifying to Teach (QtT) standards, giving it parity with 'entry requirements' and requirements for 'Training and Assessment' and 'Quality Assurance' (DfES & TTA, 2002). The aim of the partnership requirement is 'to ensure that schools are full partners in Initial Teacher Training in every way ... [contributing] to the delivery of training, [and participating] in planning, training and in selecting and assessing trainees' (TTA, 2003, p. 85). In the postgraduate certificate in education (PGCE) primary programme of 38 weeks, at least 18 weeks must be spent in school; for all secondary and Key Stage (KS) 2-3 programmes 24 weeks; for all two-, three- or four-year undergraduate programmes a minimum of 32 weeks. For PGCE programmes approximately half of the preparation of new teachers takes place in schools, under the guidance of school-based mentors.

During the 1990s the control of teacher education shifted from higher education institutions (HEIs) and local education authorities (LEAs) into the hands of centralised legislative bodies. In 1994, the TTA was established to organise, fund and determine the shape of ITT in England, and of research and higher education degrees in education. It was also at this point that ITT became officially designated as initial teacher *training*, rather than initial teacher *education* (ITE). This dissociation of ITT from higher education has been further pronounced by an increasing variety of routes into teaching through school-based graduate training programmes, overseas teacher training programmes and the separation of the award of QTS from the award of PGCE. Teachers can now enter the profession with a first degree, or equivalent, and QTS, without the postgraduate element of teacher education. Similarly, many bachelor of education programmes have been reduced from four to three years and, in some cases, two years, with the focus for entry to the profession being upon meeting the standards for QTS rather than the study of education. HEIs were also redefined, being referred to by the TTA as 'providers' along with 'providers' of QTS-based routes into teaching.

The development of education policy in the 1990s reflects a technical view of teaching focusing upon the delivery of a National Curriculum through recommended schemes of work devised by the Qualifications and Curriculum Authority, national strategies which prescribe in detail how numeracy and literacy should be delivered at KS1 (5- to 7-year-olds) and KS2 (7- to 11-year-olds) and a national strategy prescribing how key skills should be incorporated into the curriculum at KS3 (11- to 14-year-olds). At the same time a new 'standards framework' was developed to restructure the profession and to provide a basis for performance management systems and performance-related pay (DfEE, 1998). Evaluation of teacher performance against relevant national standards was established for all areas of the profession from ITT through to headteacher training. Such developments have resulted in strong pressure today to make ITT a simpler, more direct, apprenticeship system concerned with technical delivery and the development of teaching skills. Whilst subject knowledge in relation to the National Curriculum remains a policy focus for teacher education, little explicit reference is made to the knowledge of teaching and learning and the understanding of pedagogy.

The prescriptive nature of legislation governing teaching and ITT programmes has also resulted in a decrease in teacher autonomy and what has been referred to by critics as 'deprofessionalisation' (Ozga, 1995; Lawn, 1997). The increasing complexity of statutory curriculum and assessment frameworks, and the increasing diversity of the teacher's role through initiatives such as the inclusion of children with special educational needs in mainstream schooling, meant that individual teacher autonomy prevented the profession from responding effectively to new initiatives during the late 1980s. In particular, teachers' responses to change were not co-ordinated with the responses of their colleagues, leading to fragmented and inconsistent practice in relation to frameworks which required uniformity. However, autonomy is not only a necessary condition for professional behaviour, it is also necessary to being an effective practitioner:

> as professionals work in uncertain situations in which judgement is more important than routine, it is essential to effective practice that they should be sufficiently free from bureaucratic and political constraints to act on judgements made in the best interests (as they see them) of the clients. (Hoyle & John, 1995, p. 77)

The issue of autonomy was further compounded by the creation of the Office for Standards in Education (Ofsted) to inspect the compliance of schools and ITT providers in delivering policy. Rather than having control of curriculum content, pedagogy and assessment, teachers have become managers of centralised curricula and testing regimes which are subject to external surveillance. This standards-led view of the professional teacher stresses compliance, efficiency and high-quality teaching as defined and measured by external criteria. This view derives from managerialist agendas where accountability is equated with compliance with imposed and heavily regulated policies. Alternative views of the professional teacher stress the need for autonomy (Hoyle & John, 1995), and the scope to focus upon the needs and interests of pupil learning and to improve the conditions in which this can occur (Sachs, 2003). This latter view derives from democratic agendas and the belief that teachers are primarily concerned with creating and putting into place standards and processes that give pupils democratic experiences. It is somewhat ironic that the rhetoric of 'inclusion' which has been dominant in policy since the 1990s should itself be contained in managerialist frameworks which, in their attempt to standardise, can contribute to social exclusion. The introduction of school 'league tables', competitive bidding for funding, competition between teachers for personal enhancement and the recognition of 'excellence' in teaching further conflict with processes of social cohesion and inclusion.

### Partnership for Education or Training?

The statutory requirements for partnership in general are concerned with the management of partnership, compliance, quality assurance and the moderation of assessments. It is notable that reference is made to providers working with schools and everyone in them, but no specific acknowledgement is given to the specific role of the mentor. The role has not been seen as integral to the approach to teaching and professionalism. A recent move by the DfES to develop a set of standards for mentoring signals a change to this view, but it is still a long way from recognising the role of the mentor as central to the task of transforming the teaching profession (Fullan & Hargreaves, 2000).

Whilst providers have the responsibility to make sure the partnership between provider, school and LEA works effectively (DfES & TTA, 2002), all partners should be involved in making a planned, integrated contribution to the training programme (TTA, 2003). Providers have responsibility for setting up partnership agreements which outline clear roles and responsibilities for each element of training and assessment and which make clear how the elements fit together to ensure that training addresses all the standards. Providers also have responsibility for ensuring that all staff involved in training are fully prepared for, and supported in, their role.

The aim of the requirement on time in school is 'to ensure that trainee teachers have sufficient high-quality experience to enable them to demonstrate that they meet the Standards' (TTA, 2003, p. 79) What constitutes a sufficiently 'high-quality' experience or demonstration of meeting the standards can be contentious. The QtT handbook of guidance serves as an interpretive medium, describing both the scope of each standard and the relevant evidence for meeting it. For example, Standard 2.1 states that:

> Those awarded QTS must demonstrate that they have a secure
> knowledge of the subject(s) they are trained to teach. (For
> secondary trainees this needs to be equivalent to degree level.)
> (TTA, 2003, p. 14)

The handbook of guidance describes the scope of this standard as 'a high level of subject knowledge and understanding relevant to the pupil's curriculum' in order that trainees can break concepts and ideas down and plan lessons which support learning. Evidence of meeting this standard includes such things as presenting complex ideas, communicating subject knowledge, correcting pupils' errors and answering subject-based questions confidently. Whilst the guidance acknowledges a link between subject knowledge, planning and pupil learning, it does not refer to pedagogic subject knowledge, to understanding how children learn and make sense of what is taught or to understanding how the National Curriculum has been developed and that it could be contestable. The nature of the 'high-quality' experience and evidence of meeting the standard are open to more than an interpretation of what supports pupil learning or what an appropriate and effective breakdown of concepts might look like in practice. It is further open to being interpreted from the perspective of training new teachers or from the perspective of educating them.

How mentors are developed to fulfil their role depends upon whether teachers are viewed as skilled technicians or as knowledgeable professionals and whether preparation for teaching is seen as a process of training or education. The QtT standards (DfES & TTA, 2002), and criteria for TTA funding for subject support sessions for PGCE trainees in English, maths and science, support the view that trainees need to be educated in their subject studies but only need to be trained in their preparation for teaching:

> Skilled practitioners can make teaching look easy but they
> have learned their skills through training, practice, evaluation
> and by learning from other colleagues. (DfES & TTA, 2002,
> p. 2)

However, the QtT standards also state that:

> teaching involves a lot more than care, mutual respect and
> well placed optimism. It demands knowledge, practical skills,
> the ability to make informed judgements, and to balance
> pressures and challenges, practice and creativity, interest and
> effort, as well as an understanding of how children learn and
> develop. (DfES & TTA, 2002, p. 2)

Preparation for teaching involves more than knowing what is statutory, and becoming familiar with procedures to implement national policies relating to such things as inclusion, curriculum, assessment and learning. Trainees also need to understand the contexts in which they teach and the principles and theoretical constructs underlying policy if they are to make 'informed judgements' about its execution and meet the needs of the particular learners in their classrooms. As Richards (2002) argues, teachers can be trained in some aspects of their role, but they need to be educated to make informed judgements, balance pressures and challenges, develop creativity and appreciate the complex nature of teaching and learning.

In considering the recent history and current context of teacher preparation, it is argued that statutory requirements need to be interpreted from the perspective of teacher education, rather than training, in order to best serve new teachers and the children they teach. Given that approximately half of the preparation of new teachers takes place in schools under the guidance of school-based mentors, there has to be a mutual recognition of the partnership in initial teacher education between HEIs and LEAs/schools. For these partnerships to be 'effective', they need to have the professional autonomy to educate rather than train and mentors need to be empowered to be agents for change and development in the education system. To be democratic, partnerships also need to have the professional autonomy to be responsive to local 'client' needs. Whilst partnerships can operate on democratic principles and can add some pedagogic value to what statutory policy, in its rhetoric, intends to be instructional, the scope for achieving this is curtailed by the regulatory nature of Ofsted and the competitive basis for funding.

### Initial Teacher Education Partnerships and Communities of Practice

The work of Lave & Wenger (1991) situates the learning of trainees in 'communities of practice'. This perspective focuses on the relationship between the learner and the context or culture within which they learn. Through a process of 'legitimate peripheral participation', learners appropriate the meanings and actions used by more experienced and expert members of the community, and gradually increase their engagement with the complexity and practices of the community. Full participation in the community involves an ability to engage with the demands of the community and to contribute to its continuous development. Dialogue and social interaction support the learner in knowing how to proceed and in constructing understanding and ways of knowing that are specific to the community:

> The community of practice is a set of relations among persons,
> activity, and world, over time and in relation with other
> tangential and overlapping communities of practice. A
> community of practice is an intrinsic condition for the
> existence of knowledge, not least because it provides the
> interactive support necessary for making sense of its heritage.
> Thus, participation in the cultural practice in which any
> knowledge exists is an epistemological principle of learning.
> (Lave & Wenger, 1991, p. 98)

Learning to teach involves knowing about teaching and knowing the theoretical collective knowledge of the community of practice in education. It also involves knowing how to teach and the skills of the community. Traditionally, it was the role of HEI-based tutors to support trainees' knowledge and understanding of practical principles, and disciplinary theory, whilst school-based mentors were more concerned with supporting knowledge and understanding in relation to practice. Whilst this may still be true up to a point, it can be argued that these two kinds of knowledge need to be kept in close contact for two important reasons:

> First, knowledge about teaching can only be developed in
> ways that are relevant to the improvement of education if it
> develops out of the needs and insights of the whole education
> community and is developed and tested in that community.
> Secondly, our understanding of the relationship between
> understanding and skill...tells us that the complex skill of
> teaching is an informed skill and not a string of unthinkingly
> applied procedures. (Edwards & Collison, 1996, p. 18)

Trainees need opportunities to make sense of knowledge about teaching and learning and to understand the theoretical underpinnings of pedagogy in their school-based experience, as well as through HEI-based teaching, if they are to develop an understanding of pupil learning. In order to support coherent and progressive learning, the partnership between schools and the HEI needs to be established on the basis of a community of practice for ITE where roles, responsibilities, knowledge and skills are shared, and where there is equal partnership in the development and delivery of ITE. To this end Edwards & Collison (1996) present a Vygotskian framework for training partnerships.

This framework derives from a sociocultural theory of learning based on the ideas of Vygotsky. From this view learning is seen as an interaction between the learner's previous experience and perceptions of the world, and new experiences and ideas. Learners construct ideas and understanding rather than receiving them complete and correct from authoritative sources. Cultural meanings of the community are shared through interaction within the social group then internalised by the individual. New ideas are introduced in the public arena of the HEI or school, then fitted into the individual's current structures of knowledge and belief in private or semi-private settings. Learners then 'try out' their new knowledge or skill in a public arena. Here a teacher or mentor can formatively assess the degree of understanding and learners can contribute to how knowledge is structured and used in the community. School-based mentors need to be able to support trainees to move from peripheral to full participation in the community of the school as well as in teaching, through this learning process.

Moving from peripheral to full participation in the community of mentor practice is more difficult. Mentors can be supported through courses by the partner HEI, but these are often dominated by the need to implement assessment and other course procedures, leaving little time to focus upon mentor learning and development. Mentors may be supported by more experienced mentors in their school but this is more likely to result in an induction to mentor practice in the school rather than the mentor community. Mentors may also be supported by visits from HEI tutors or more experienced mentors from other schools, but constraints of time and funding limit the scope and quality of support visiting tutors and mentors can give. In practice, new mentors have to participate fully in their role from the start, with very little support or guidance. They have to learn by doing, often in relative isolation, and manage their own learning. For mentors to become full participating members of a community of mentor practice there need to be more opportunities for them to be exposed to new ideas, and to construct and reconstruct their knowledge and skills in the public arena.

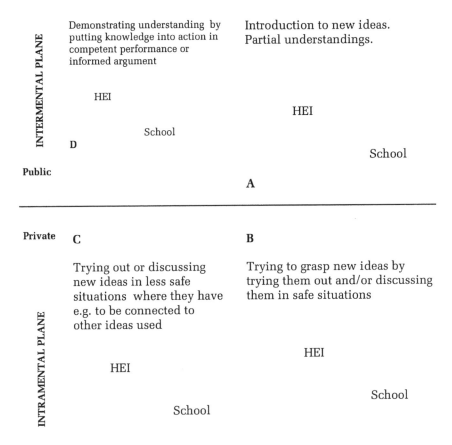

Figure 1. A Vygotskian framework for training with partnership.

## The Impact of Beliefs and Perspectives on Learning

It has been well documented that trainees' beliefs about teaching based on previous experience and perceptions of education have a significant influence on learning to teach (Cole & Knowles, 1993; Elliott & Calderhead, 1995; Edwards & Collison, 1996). Existing knowledge, experience and beliefs need to be recognised and challenged in order to support the trainee in reconstructing and developing them appropriately in the light of new ideas and experiences. If existing constructions are not challenged, they can remain stable over time, despite new experiences and ideas, and can impede development. Furthermore, challenging trainee constructs of teaching is an ongoing process in moving their learning on throughout their development as teachers (Day, 1999). In order to support trainee learning, mentors need to understand and engage in the process of challenge, and help trainees refine or amend their perceptions as appropriate.

Similarly, mentors hold pre-defined ideas about their role and bring their own particular orientations and conceptualisations to the mentoring task (Elliott & Calderhead, 1995; Saunders et al, 1995). These orientations tend to be on a general level rather than specific to the mentor role and reflect simplistic views about learning to teach. Mentors tend to behave as if it is unproblematic and uncontentious to implement recommended good practice (Haggerty, 1995), and do not recognise or articulate the complexity of decisions teachers make. There is also a sense in which mentors and trainees collude towards a position of safety. Trainees tend to see themselves as 'polite guests' rather than learners, in classrooms, and offer tasks that can be implemented smoothly (Edwards & Collison, 1996). Mentors tend to be concerned about disruption to behaviour in the class, and delivery of the curriculum. This results in conversations with the trainee which are mainly concerned with practical strategies for behaviour management and instructions for the implementation of the curriculum. These are real concerns to mentors, who are themselves accountable through pupil performance in national tests, Ofsted inspection and performance management systems. In this context, mentors are more likely to be concerned with the trainee's performance and delivery of the curriculum than with challenging their constructs and developing their learning.

Challenge between mentors and trainees, and between HEI-based tutors and mentors, relies upon the capacity to build trusting and open relationships. Research by Brooks (1996) reports that mentors gave highest priority to interpretational skills and the interpersonal elements of the relationship they establish with trainees, over personal qualities, professional skills and subject-specific expertise. Other authors note the centrality of relationships as a source for trainee learning about teaching (Bennet & Carre, 1993; Elliott & Calderhead, 1995; Hawkey, 1998). There is more likely to be tolerance of challenge from friends than from strangers or enemies, and good relationships foster change. An ability to form close and honest relationships is important if mentors, tutors and trainees are to be agents of change.

*Helen Mitchell*

## From Legitimate Peripheral Participation to Full Participation

Maynard & Furlong (1995) describe five stages in the process of learning to teach, which offer a view of the movement from legitimate peripheral participation to full participation: early idealism, survival, recognising difficulties, hitting the plateau and moving on. As trainees progress through these stages, the focus of their learning changes. Initial stages are characterised by a need to know and understand rules and routines, to establish authority and to understand how to observe an experienced teacher and make sense of what is gong on in the classroom. This is followed by a focus on developing teaching competence, where the trainee is mainly concerned with adopting types of behaviour that will lead to positive assessments against the standards. It is at this point that that trainees can 'hit a plateau' and need to be challenged to move on from 'acting like a teacher' to 'thinking like a teacher'. The moving-on stage is crucial in that trainees shift their focus of attention from themselves as teachers to children as learners, and to the development of effective teaching for learning. Maynard & Furlong (1995) conceptualise three models of mentoring for different stages of trainee development:

1. the apprenticeship model, where trainees can 'learn to see' through working alongside a mentor who can explain the significance of what is happening in the classroom and where the mentor can model established routines and practice;
2. the competency model, where the mentor takes on the role of a systematic trainer, observing the trainee, allowing them to take control of the teaching process and learn by initially adopting some of the mentor's ready-made routines and progressing to form and implement some of their own whilst continually developing and modifying their constructs of education;
3. the reflective model, where trainees move beyond routines and rituals to develop a deeper understanding of the learning process, think through different ways of teaching and develop their own justifications and practical principles from their work, and where the mentor becomes a co-enquirer into practice.

Each model is 'partial and inadequate, perhaps only appropriate at a particular stage of a trainee's development...[but] taken together they may contribute to a view of mentoring that responds to the changing needs of trainees' (Maynard & Furlong, 1995, p. 17). Whilst this model is idealised and does not take account of the personal and idiosyncratic nature of trainee development, it is useful for helping mentors to understand their role in relation to trainee learning, and as a framework for challenging and exploring their own practice. In the context of today's schools, trainees are given few real opportunities for peripheral participation. The pressure to cover a wide and detailed curriculum and the prescriptive nature of national strategies leave little flexibility in how whole-class teaching and group work are managed and organised. Mentors also tend to rush trainees into teaching as a way of learning to teach. The pressure for trainees to cover their own curriculum and collect evidence of meeting the standards, combined with the mentor's accountability for their own performance, mitigate against opportunities for reflection and challenging enquiry.

### Mentor Education

Mentor education programmes need to establish a community of practice in which mentors and trainees can learn. To do this they need to establish a culture of practice which views the mentor role as a way of educating new teachers to become autonomous professionals, and in which mentors view themselves as autonomous pedagogical partners in the ITE process. There also need to be opportunities for mentors and HEI-based tutors to establish open and trusting relationships. In the context of inadequate funding opportunities for mentor education, and in the context of managerialist policies, where teacher educators, mentors and schools are all constrained in the degree of professional autonomy they can exercise, this presents a difficult challenge.

In response to this challenge, a developmental mentor education programme has been created at the University of East London (UEL), for mentors of primary PGCE trainees. The programme is based around a framework for mentor education developed by the London Providers (LP) mentor group, which consists of tutors from a range of London HEIs and a school-based provider. The LP framework consists of outcomes for three stages of mentor development, and aims to provide a structure which is coherently progressive, and which will bring parity to the provision of mentor education across London. The outcomes are intended to be used as a guide to the stages of mentor development and not as performance indicators. The LP framework is underpinned by a pedagogy derived from Lave & Wenger's (1991) view of learning through communities of practice, and socio-constructivist principles of learning.

The UEL programme provides opportunities for all mentors to attend one day of mentor education at the HEI, each school term (three days a year), with reimbursement to the school to cover their absence. New mentors attend an additional day in the first term as part of their induction to the mentor community of practice. Mentors at stage 3 may be engaged in activities for up to five days a year depending upon the needs and opportunities within the community, and funding. Mentors normally operate at stages 1 and 2 for a year each before moving on to stage 3.

The aims of the programme are to:

1. support coherent and progressive learning, across the partnership;

2. provide opportunities for mentors to be exposed to new ideas, and to construct and reconstruct their knowledge and skills in the public arena;
3. support mentors to understand and engage in the process of challenging trainees' constructs to develop their learning;
4. provide opportunities for mentors to develop open and trusting relationships within the mentor community of practice and to contribute to the development of the community.

At stage 1, mentors are introduced to the role and education focuses upon:

- evaluating practice;
- proposing areas of development;
- observing and analysing practice;
- suggesting changes in classroom strategies;
- re-evaluating the effects of change.

At stage 2, there is a focus upon:

- articulating the principles and procedures of teaching practice, to become empowered to undertake active and professional responsibility for teaching the trainee;
- reflecting upon the differences between how mentors say they operate/would choose to operate, and how they do operate;
- understanding how trainees learn, and exploring the relationship between the mentor role and trainee development;
- understanding the need for balance between support and challenge, and how to achieve this in practice.

Stage 3 focuses upon using the knowledge and skills developed at stages 1 and 2, to support other less experienced mentors, and to understand mentor development. Mentors at stage 3 of the programme attend fewer whole-group sessions and have the following choices of how they will spend the rest of their (minimum) three-day entitlement.

- *Supporting new mentors* – three/five visits to stage 1/2 mentors over the year, to offer support, carry out joint observation of and feedback for trainees, support planning, evaluation and review meetings with trainees and model challenging practice.
- *Supporting schools new to ITE* – working with teachers in schools which are new to ITE or in schools which wish to develop policy and practice in this area.
- *Mentor education* – working alongside HEI-based tutors either individually or in small teams to develop and deliver stage 1 and 2 mentor education.

- *Resource development* – working alongside HEI-based tutors, or in mentor working parties, to develop mentor support materials and to review and develop course procedures and documentation.
- *Master's level enquiry* – undertaking a 30-credit master's level module in mentoring and coaching during their three education days; and they are entitled to two free modules in total on the MA in Education and Development programme.

The programme aims to address some of the concerns raised in this chapter in the following ways.

- Mentor education sessions focus predominantly on their learning, rather than the implementation of procedures.
- New and less experienced mentors are supported in implementing procedures by more experienced mentors, through working together in practice. This frees up more learning time in their education sessions, and provides opportunities for mentors to make meaningful links between theory and practice.
- Opportunities for mentors to work across the community of practice, in each other's schools, and to learn in the public as well as private arena, are maximised.
- Education sessions are interactive, introduce new ideas and research and challenge mentors' constructs about how trainees learn, and about their own development and practice as mentors.

Whilst this programme moves some way towards addressing some of the issues outlined in this chapter, relatively little can be achieved through three days' education a year and a few inter-school visits. Mentors also have to juggle their role with many other competing demands and responsibilities, and regularly have to engage in training for new government initiatives and local responses to them. Setting up learning activities in mentor education sessions which can be undertaken in school and then brought back to the community to be used as basis for further learning is not generally realistic as a goal. For example, mentors could keep a learning log or reflective journal, plan and carry out school-based research or engage with reading a wider range of research and ideas. To sustain learning from this kind of approach there need to be more frequent opportunities for interaction, feedback and discussion within the community than once a term. Often it is difficult for mentors just to attend the HEI-based education days and fulfil the bare requirements of their role in school. Given the complexity of the mentor role, opportunities and funding for education and support are not adequate and certainly do not reflect the fact that mentors in schools are responsible for *c.* 50% of the training of new teachers.

There is also a limit to the impact that mentor education can have when mentors, schools and HEIs have statutory obligations to be delivers of a curriculum, and are accountable to imposed and heavily regulated managerialist policies. For mentors to be empowered as full participators in the community of mentoring, and to engage as equal partners in the ITE process, they need to have the professional autonomy to be more than skilled technicians bounded by compliance.

## References

Bennet, N. & Carre, C. (1993) *Learning to Teach*. London: Routledge.

Brooks, V. (1996) Mentoring: the interpersonal dimension, *Teacher Development*, 1, pp. 5-10.

Cole, A.L. & Knowles, J.G. (1993) Shattered Images: understanding expectations and realities of field experience, *Teaching and Teacher Education*, 9(5-6), pp. 457-471.

Day, C. (1999) *Developing Teachers: the challenges of lifelong learning*. London: Falmer Press.

Department for Education and Employment (DfEE) (1998) *Teachers: meeting the challenge of change*. London: DfEE.

Department for Education and Science (1984) *Circular 3/84. Initial Teacher Training: approval of courses*. London: HMSO.

Department for Education and Skills & Teacher Training Agency (DfES & TTA) (2002) *Qualifying to Teach: professional standards for Qualified Teacher Status and requirements for Initial Teacher Training*. London: DfES & TTA.

Edwards, A. & Collison, J. (1996) *Mentoring and Developing Practice in Primary Schools: supporting student teacher learning in schools*. Buckingham: Open University Press.

Elliott, B. & Calderhead, J. (1995) Mentoring for Teacher Development: possibilities and caveats, in T. Kerry & A. Shelton-Mayes (Eds) *Issues in Mentoring*. London: Routledge in association with the Open University.

Fullan, M. & Hargreaves, A. (2000) Mentoring in the New Millennium, *Theory into Practice*, 39(1), pp. 50-56.

Haggerty, L. (1995) The Use of Content Analysis to Explore Conversations between School Teacher Mentors and Student Teachers, *British Educational Research Journal*, 21(2), pp. 183-187.

Hawkey, K. (1998) Mentor Pedagogy and Student Teacher Professional Development: a study of two mentoring relationships, *Teaching and Teacher Education*, 14(6), pp. 657-670.

Hoyle, E. & John, P.D. (1995) *Professional Knowledge and Professional Practice*. London: Cassell.

Lave, J. & Wenger, E. (1991) *Situated Learning: legitimate peripheral participation*. Cambridge: Cambridge University Press.

Lawn, M. (1997) *Modern Times? Work, Professionalism and Citizenship in Teaching*. London: Falmer Press.

Maynard, T. & Furlong, J. (1995) Learning to Teach and Models of Mentoring, in T. Kerry & A. Shelton-Mayes (Eds) *Issues in Mentoring*. London: Routledge in association with the Open University.

Ozga, J. (1995) Deskilling a Profession: professionalism, deprofessionalism and the new managerialism, in H. Busher & R. Saran (Eds) *Managing Teachers as Professionals in Schools*. London: Kogan Page.

Richards, C. (2002) Preparing to Become a Primary School Teacher: changing the standards? in N. Simco & T. Wilson (Eds) *Primary Initial Training and Education: revised standards bright future?* Exeter: Learning Matters.

Sachs, J. (2003) *The Activist Professional*. Buckingham: Open University Press.

Saunders, S., Pettinger, K. & Tomlinson, P. (1995) Prospective Mentors' Views on Partnership in Secondary Teacher Training, *British Educational Research Journal*, 21(2), pp. 199-219.

Teacher Training Agency (TTA) (2003) *Qualifying to Teach: handbook of guidance*. London: TTA.

CHAPTER 3

# Mentor Professional Development in Portugal

## IRENE FIGUEIREDO

### Introduction: the context of teacher training

To fully understand the situation of teacher training in Portugal today reference must be made to the political and social evolution of the country in the last 30 years. Until April 1974, under a long-lasting (48 years) right-wing authoritarian regime, the Portuguese education system was organised into four years of primary education (six- to 10-years-old) and two more years of preparatory education (10- to 12-years-old), which together constituted compulsory education, and five years, later on (1977) six years, of a two-stream secondary education: *liceu*, grammar school. The more elitist of these had the main purpose of educating those who could aspire to university and/or to be selected for medium-status public administration jobs. The technical school was of lower social standing, for those who did not succeed in the selective grammar school entrance examinations, but could continue studying. The technical schools stream prepared a skilled workforce for the industrial and commercial sectors. The enrolment rate in post-compulsory education was very low: 57% in 1985 (UNESCO, 1995). There were many drop-outs and much failure and overall underachievement even in the preparatory cycle, i.e. even during the compulsory education period. Higher education was reduced to university – in Lisbon, Coimbra and Porto. In 1970 the enrolment rate was 5% (Arroteia, 1996). After the expansion resulting from the creation of the so-called new universities by the Education Act 1973 this rate increased to 10.8% in 1984-85.

Primary education was taught in separate schools, the *escola primária*, with one teacher for each group/class of pupils. The preparatory cycle (fifth and sixth form) was taught in separate preparatory schools. In spite of being a part of compulsory education (since 1966), the curriculum of the preparatory education maintained a subject-based organisation. The strong academic character of such programmes underlined the similarity with secondary education.

In secondary education the institutional differentiation of the two streams prevailed in Portugal until 1975. In the second half of the 1970s, under the new democratic regime, these three years, although still not compulsory, underwent unification. The intention was to organise them, as in most European countries, according to the comprehensive principle, bearing in mind that this was considered to be a more favourable model for school democratisation in accordance with more egalitarian educational policies. However, this was only a nominal change as it was not accompanied by the restructuring either of school buildings, equipment and didactic materials or of the necessary teacher training. It is therefore widely recognised that in practice the model that prevailed after that unification was the grammar school (*liceu*) model. This was the model all the prestige social representations were associated with and for that reason succeeded in overpowering the principles of the comprehensive school. As a result, the unified secondary education developed an academic subject-based curriculum somehow like a grammar school education for all, thus becoming the failure of many.

These models of preparatory and secondary education were to last until the introduction of basic education by Education Law 46/86, of 14 October 1986, in both structure and organisation.

### Initial Teacher Training: early approaches

Primary schoolteachers and later on also nursery educators had non-higher initial training at specialised training institutions, the *escolas do magistério primário*, based upon an integrated model. These were the only teaching staff to have an initial professional training programme since the nineteenth century, when several *escolas normais* (normal schools) were founded in the main cities of the country.

The preparatory schoolteacher training model was similar to the training of secondary schoolteachers: most obtained a university degree, which was later followed by pedagogic professional in-service training. During almost the entire period of the authoritarian regime, *liceu* and technical schoolteachers had a very restrictive professional training and most of them could be working a lifetime without becoming professional teachers. After obtaining a university degree in one scientific domain they had to follow a course on pedagogic sciences at the faculties of humanities of the universities of Lisbon, Porto or Coimbra, and a practicum period of two years teaching at one of the three normal grammar schools, or at certain specially appointed technical schools. To be admitted to this practical component of training, candidates had to succeed in a very selective examination. Only a few places were available every year and trainees were not paid during those two years. The training programme was only complete after the trainee succeeded in the Exame de Estado (State Exam).

Underlying this model was the partnership between schools, the educational authorities, i.e. the Ministry of Education, as schools were all public, and the university. Mentors were experienced and reliable grammar schoolteachers working together with university professors. It would last more or less untouched from the 1930s until around 1970, when the increase in preparatory and secondary school enrolments required more trained teaching staff and an adequate number of practicum places. Bearing in mind that more than 90% of the Portuguese schools are state-owned and -ruled, this anachronistic situation meant a lot of unfairness because only after training could teachers obtain professional qualification and the right to apply for a permanent job as a civil servant. (In 1971 the faculties of science of the three universities launched a new model of their own, the so-called 'educational option' integrating a scientific component, educational subjects and practice.)

In 1974, soon after the revolution, crucial changes in teacher training were introduced: the selective examinations, namely for entrance one and the State Exam, were abolished, the practicum was reduced to one year and the number of schools to carry it out was considerably increased. This meant also the end of the partnership with the universities and greater responsibility for mentors. In fact, by that time the Ministry of Education controlled the whole training process, including the appointment of practicum schools, mentor training and the selection of trainees. Mentors used to meet on a regional and national basis to discuss issues such as trainee evaluation criteria and standards. With some changes in 1979 this model would last until the approval of the Education Law of 1986 that would bring a shift towards the prevalence of higher education institutions (HEIs) in initial teacher training (ITT).

Until 1985-86 *escolas do magistério primário* carried out primary teachers' and nursery educators' initial training as non-higher education. From that time on polytechnic schools of education took charge of nursery educators' and first- and second-cycle basic schoolteachers' initial training at higher education level.

## Structure and Ordering of the Portuguese Education System

*Education Law 46/86 of 14 October 1986, Lei de Bases do Sistema Educativo (Amended by Education Law 115/97 of 19 September)*

By increasing the duration of compulsory education to nine years, the 1986 Lei de Bases do Sistema Educativo (LBSE) had a double purpose. The first was to promote a strong change in the nature of compulsory education by defining it as basic to all individuals, with independent aims of its own. These aims included the acquisition of knowledge, skills and attitudes that constitute the basis both for continuing a formal education and for further acquisitions in life-long learning. The second purpose was to prepare for entering work life. The LBSE realised the notion of mass schooling based on the principle of 'an education for all'. This meant an intention to organise the nine years of compulsory basic education according to the integrated model in force in Denmark, for example. The law defined three cycles, consisting of the first cycle of basic education (first to fourth form), the second cycle (fifth and sixth form) and the third cycle (seventh, eighth and ninth form), respectively.

Until today, however, the successful implementation of basic education has not been achieved. The new structure of cycles has not corresponded sufficiently with the previous structures for primary, preparatory and secondary unified education, and neither has the new structure promoted the necessary ruptures with previous assumptions and practices for it to become established. Separate schools are maintained for each of the three cycles of basic education, as the first cycle is still being taught at primary schools, totally separate from the second-cycle schools. These have progressively come to include also the third cycle (EB2, 3). However, the third cycle is still also being taught at secondary schools. Despite some attempts at organisational integration, namely through the grouping of schools of the three cycles of basic education placed in the same neighbourhood, they are in fact very different realities.

### ITT at HEIs

The LBSE of 1986 (together with its amendment in 1997) established, for the first time, an initial training system for teachers of all school levels, whilst recognising distinct institutions for the initial training of basic education teachers:

- the schools of education (*escola superior de educação*) of the polytechnic higher education subsystem (*institutos politécnicos*) to train teachers for the first and second cycles of basic education and also nursery educators;
- the universities to train teachers for the third cycle of basic education and for secondary education.

The universities, having an integrated teachers' education unit, specifically for that purpose, may also train nursery educators and teachers for the first and second cycles of basic education. Despite establishing a higher education-level training for all teachers and nursery educators, in its first version of 1986 the law distinguishes between the bachelor's degree, *bacharelato* (nursery educators and teachers of the first cycle of basic education), and the licence degree, *licenciatura* (second and third cycles of basic education teachers and of secondary education teachers).

The amendment to the LBSE (1997) introduced some changes, namely: (1) *licenciatura*-level training (four to five years at HEIs) for all teachers and nursery educators; and (2) schools of education being granted competence to train also the third cycle of basic education teachers. These decisions had the intention to revise the initial project in order to give more coherence to basic education according to a unified integrated model. However, the new responsibility of the schools of education in the global and integrated training of teachers for the three cycles of basic education never came into force, as this amendment to the Education Law has never been regulated. Therefore the training of teachers for the third cycle of basic education together with secondary schoolteacher training is still exclusively at universities.

This is another indicator that the basic education identity that has been imposed by law on the seventh, eighth and ninth form, in the absence of concomitant changes in other dimensions of the education system, could never become a reality. In fact the subject-based curricular structure established for this cycle, the teacher profile and the respective initial training system keep it clearly as a secondary education level even when compulsory.

### Organisation of Initial Training
### Components – the integrated model

The LBSE of 1986 (together with its amendment in 1997) settles the general principles of teacher training.

The general principles for training educators and teachers (LBSE, article 30) applying to all non-higher educational levels demonstrate a clear will to implement an integrated model of ITT 'both in terms of scientific-pedagogical training and coordination between theory and practice' (article 30, 1-d ). While stressing the need for ITT to develop the future teacher's 'personal and social training appropriate to carrying out their function' (article 30, 1-a ), the law establishes a teacher training programme which 'stimulates a simultaneously critical and active attitude to social realities' (article 30, 1-f ), 'encourages and stimulates innovation and research, particularly in relation to education' (article 30, 1-g) and provides 'participatory training which leads to reflexive and continued practice of self-information and self-learning' (article 30, 1-h).

In synthesis it can be recognised that the Portuguese legal framework for ITT is based upon the principles and approaches that underlie most ITT systems nowadays in Europe, namely the broader notion of teacher education as professionalisation:

> The main components of a professionalised teacher education
> programme might be:

– studies in the sciences of the teaching profession (e.g. educational sciences, *Didaktik/Fachdidaktik* literally translated as didactics and subject matter didactics, educational psychology, educational sociology),
– all of these closely connected to educational research and aiming at the development of
– professional problem-solving capacity,
– a broad repertoire of validated practices to promote and support learning, and
– a professional code of ethics. Other components are:
– coherent and supervised practical and /or clinical studies,
– in depth studies in a number of academic fields relevant for curricula of schools and teaching, studying and learning particular cases and/or topics, and
– an integration of studies in the sciences of the teaching profession, other academic studies and clinical and/or practical studies would also form part of such programme.
(Buchberger et al, 2000, p. 19)

Reforms of teacher education all over developed countries including Portugal work along this line. In fact the Portuguese ITT system, at least in the rhetoric of its legal framework, follows current research findings to inform what it outlines as training components, and its organisation of the training curriculum. There are also similarities with other European countries when offering different models: one for training primary and lower secondary education teachers and another for secondary education teachers. Portugal follows a similar model to other countries, where primary and lower secondary teachers are trained in accordance with the model of integration of the training components, and secondary teachers according to a variety of options, including the integrated model but also the consecutive one with a first basis of academic subject-centred training, followed by training on education science, specific didactics and supervised practice. In Portugal, as in most European countries, there is now this diversity of models for the third cycle of basic education and for secondary education. For some vocational and artistic areas teacher training as in-service training is still the only possibility. However, all these models allow the polytechnic or university HEI to have control of the training. Moreover as this is mainly a 'one-phase' model, i.e. 'the successful completion of initial teacher education at institutions of teacher education permits the (prospective) teacher to apply for a post at schools' (Buchberger et al, 2000, annex), higher education teacher training institutions have the power of delivering certificates with a double value: as an academic graduation diploma, and as a professional credential.

### The Control of Initial Teacher Education

In spite of the strongly centralised and uniform model that defines the Portuguese education system, HEIs, polytechnic and university, enjoy full autonomy, even when compared to those countries that have traditionally decentralised systems. Along with some national guidelines, higher education ITT institutions, polytechnic schools of education and universities, do enjoy considerable autonomy in the design, development and assessment of their training programmes. Thus, in what constitutes initial training, the training components defined nation-wide are those currently enforced in other countries: education sciences, scientific disciplines, specific didactics and pedagogic practice. Each higher education initial training institution has full responsibility for the content of these components, their organisation and the associated teaching-learning process. Regarding the relationship between them and the schools where the practice of the future teachers takes place, there are also some national frameworks and guidelines. However, in this field HEIs have significant autonomy in relation to both the services of the Ministry of Education and the cooperating schools.

According to the national legal framework, as mentioned before, the initial training model being developed at the schools of education is based on the integration of the scientific, education sciences and practice components, associating the scientific-pedagogic preparation and the articulation between theory and practice. The programmes must contemplate the development of a wide spectrum of skills involved in the different roles that the future teachers will play, including their own personal development.

The qualification obtained through the successful completion of the HEI initial training courses automatically grants its holder a professional status, thus allowing them to apply for the teachers' national board. In Portugal, the Ministry of Education places teachers at a school through a nationally organised and co-ordinated procedure.

It can therefore be concluded that in an education system characterised by its centralism, in what concerns ITT, together with the main decisions that make the entrance to the profession possible, central political and administrative authority delegates its power to the higher education sector, more precisely to each teacher training HEI.

While sharing the situation of most member states of the European Union (EU), where 'teacher education has become an integral part of the sector of higher education' and therefore 'teacher education shares both the general changes of the context of the higher sector and the challenges with which the sector is confronted' (Buchberger et al, 2000, p. 33), in Portugal this means that ITT programmes share the high degree of autonomy that the Portuguese HEIs have always been granted.

Although the assumption by the political and administrative authority of such a discrete profile guarantees the diversity and plurality of ITT pathways, on the other hand it is not exempt from risks. In fact and for some years, in the absence both of general guidelines, i.e. a common core curriculum for all ITT courses, and of the evaluation of higher education system, there was no assurance of effective training of future teachers covering all the roles they are expected to play.

To fully understand this issue reference should be made to the particular situation of private higher education in Portugal. Practically non-existent until the mid 1980s, it played a major role in the development of higher education enrolment rates. The evolution of the number of students enrolled in public and private higher education between 1985-86 and 1991-92 (Cunha, 1994) is shown in Table I.

|  | Public higher education | Private higher education | Total | Enrolment rate (relative to age group |
|---|---|---|---|---|
| 1985-86 | 91,863 | 14,609 | 106,472 | 12.4% |
| 1991-92 | 150,962 | 63,400 | 214,362 | 25.1% |
| Growth rate | 64.3% | 334% | 10.1% | |

Table I. Evolution of the number of students enrolled in public and private higher education between 1985-86 and 1991-92.

The growth of the private higher education sector continued in the following years. In the 1993-94 school year public higher education had 169,479 enrolments (126,032 in university and 43,447 in polytechnic institutions), and private higher education, including the Portuguese Catholic University, had 93,779 enrolments (32,281 in universities, 52,686 in polytechnics and 8812 in the Portuguese Catholic University) (Arroteia, 1996). According to UNESCO (1995), in 1995 the enrolment rate in private HEIs reached 34%.

Such a growth did not happen without huge difficulties, the most important being the lack of qualified professors with master's and doctoral degrees to cope with the national needs of both public and private demand (an increase of approximately 400% in 60 years – see Arroteia [1996]). This situation was particularly serious in the private sector. The solution, at least during the first part of the expansion years, was to recruit professors in the public sector who started working in both sectors.

On the other hand the high cost of the buildings and equipment to develop some higher education domains were an obstacle during those initial times so that the private supply in some areas, like health and technology, were considerably low, as the data relating to 1992-93 demonstrate (see Figure 1).

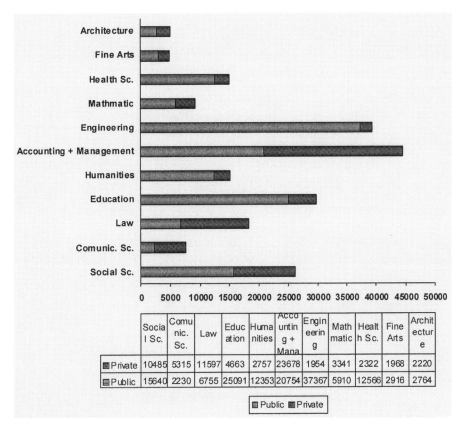

| | Social Sc. | Comunic. Sc. | Law | Education | Humanities | Accounting + Management | Engineering | Mathmatic | Health Sc. | Fine Arts | Architecture |
|---|---|---|---|---|---|---|---|---|---|---|---|
| Private | 10485 | 5315 | 11597 | 4663 | 2757 | 23678 | 1954 | 3341 | 2322 | 1968 | 2220 |
| Public | 15640 | 2230 | 6755 | 25091 | 12353 | 20754 | 37367 | 5910 | 12566 | 2916 | 2764 |

Public  Private

Figure 1. 1992-93 rates of public–private delivery across the higher education sector. Source: Departamento de Programação e Gestão Financeira (DEPGEF) (1996).

The expansion of private higher education slowed down from 1996 onwards due to the increase in public sector supply (an increase of 110% in vacancies, 74% in universities and 317% in polytechnics), the restrictive rules established through the Private Higher Education Statute and the launching of the Higher Education Evaluation System, which imposed more demanding quality standards on all HEIs, both public and private.

The expansion of the private higher education offer including the teacher training courses contributed to the high surplus of professional teachers who every year, and differently from what happens today in the developed countries, finish their initial training knowing that they will not get a job. Bearing in mind that the final quantitative qualification obtained determines the teacher's position in the list of the national competition for a job, it is understandable how important it is to assure the quality of any teacher training course, be it public or private.

As long as the control of initial teacher education belongs almost exclusively to HEIs, practice, whether in the integrated or consecutive model, and therefore the quality of mentoring, will always be the most difficult training component to be assessed even by the external evaluation committees, the only certainty being an extreme diversity of trained teachers. For example, it is up to the HEI, namely its scientific council and practice supervisors, to determine whether practice will privilege only classroom curricular activities, or whether it will also focus on other school dimensions.

In order to give a direct answer to these concerns, namely accountability and quality assurance, and beyond the general scope and aims of the Higher Education Evaluation System, there was a signal of the central authority's intention to recover the lost control, or at least a part of it, over ITT and professionalisation. This intention was made explicit through the creation in 1998 of the Instituto Nacional de Acreditação da Formação dos Professores (INAFOP) (National Institute for the Accreditation of Teacher Training). The mission of INAFOP, whose director and staff were recruited from the most prestigious and experienced higher education professors as well as basic and secondary teachers and teacher educators, was to establish stricter guidelines for teacher training courses in terms of their content, organisation and quality standards. In the short term only teacher training courses having received an accreditation by INAFOP would be entitled to grant the professional credential. Otherwise the students would only be awarded the academic graduate diploma. INAFOP began its work focusing on initial training. It prepared and submitted to public debate several working papers. In 2000 the Standards in Initial Teacher Education were published as Deliberation 1488/2000 and on 30 August 2001 the School Teacher General Teaching Profile came to light as Decree-law 240/2001, where the standards:

> Constitute a set of criteria for assessing the degree to which the programmes meet the demands of teaching performance. It is a question of generic statements, applicable to all programmes, and involves principles, objectives and conditions which should be taken into account and linked with the general profile and the specific profiles of pre-school and schoolteacher performance, the regulation of the accreditation process and the accreditation application guidelines. They focus on the following areas: 1. Programme's professional objectives, co-ordination and regulation; 2. Collaborative and partnership efforts for developing the programme; 3. Programme curriculum; 4. Selection and evaluation of trainees and professional qualification certification; 5. Teaching and non-teaching personnel and materials.

In spite of the intended regulation the decree adds:

> The standards indicate the principles, which must be
> safeguarded, and the objectives which should be reached, but
> they leave a wide margin of freedom for institutions to decide
> on how to effect them. For example, they do not prescribe in
> detail how professional practice periods, field trips and
> mechanisms for regulating the programme should be run, nor
> how to effect partnerships with schools and the educational
> administration.

This statement confirms previous arguments regarding both the high degree of autonomy of HEIs and the diversity of ITT practice, as well as the possible relationship between higher education supervisors and school mentors. Only through case studies can there be an exact representation of what is really happening.

In spite of all the innovative research and development activities of INAFOP, together with the mentioned regulatory documents, this institute was abolished in 2001. In fact, a new political coalition (central-right and right-wing) won general elections in 2002 and decided to abolish most of the institutes that had been created by the socialist government, with the argument that they constituted a parallel public administration causing resource waste and lack of motivation among officers in the public mainstream. Among HEIs, INAFOP was a controversial institution. On one hand the excellence of its work was recognised as well as the need for more regulation and accountability in the ITT system. On the other hand, however, HEIs were already coping with the Higher Education Evaluation System and, having in mind the lack of co-ordination between this system and the accreditation process of INAFOP, they were foreseeing huge amounts of time spent on both processes. So far the INAFOP mission has not been replaced. The option for two separate ministries – the Ministry of Education for the basic and secondary education system, and the new Ministry of Science, Innovation and Higher Education – may account for such a situation, furthermore, when there is an indication that the Higher Education National Evaluation System is also to be reformed.

### Some Empirical Evidence on the Role of Mentoring: the case of the School of Education of the Polytechnic Institute of Porto

In 1998, within the scope of the Thematic Network on Teacher Education in Europe (TNTEE), sponsored by the EU's Socrates programme, subnetwork B, a group of professors from the School of Education of the Polytechnic Institute of Porto (ESE/IPP), together with the team of mentors from the practice cooperating schools, in the recognition that the kind of relationship to be established between the training institutions and the cooperating schools is a decisive factor to the quality of training, decided to do a case study on this particular issue.

The study presented itself as an opportunity to respond to the needs of institutions in proceeding with an assessment of the implemented model and, simultaneously, to define a teacher education project capable of preparing future teachers for the new roles that they would be called to perform. The agreed aims of the study were:

- to identify the legal and institutional boundaries of possible collaboration;
- to identify the type and degree of existing collaboration, its constraints and potential;
- within the autonomy of the two institutions involved, to present proposals that might enable a more sharply focused collaboration in the sense of a true partnership.

Starting from the national legal norms, this confirmed the approach underlying the most significant aspects of the LBSE through explicit references to:

- the diversity of contexts and the related specific needs;
- the effective development of the educational project of the teacher education institution;
- the diversity of the teacher education situations;
- the offer of adequate training opportunities to the schools' cooperating teachers;
- the support to the educational projects of the schools where the practice takes place.

Notwithstanding, the competences ascribed to the supervisors of the teacher education institution and those ascribed to mentors in the schools are evidence of a formally institutionalised hierarchical relationship with power clearly residing with the teacher education institution. In all the documents that constitute the internal regulations of the ESE/IPP for both intra- and inter-organisational relationships, an entirely technical approach with the definition of rigidly patterned situations, roles and relationships were identified.

The hierarchical logic identified in the national legal norms is assimilated in the ESE/IPP internal rules as the teacher education institution assumes its dominant role over the schools where practice takes place.

A general conclusion from the study of these documents is that the normative function assumed by the teacher education institution is considered a far more important aim than other purposes so rhetorically evoked.

In considering the process of selecting and recruiting cooperating schools and mentors, to support the integrated model of training emphasis is placed upon the need for future teachers to have opportunities to practise which are integrated within the four years of their training and other non-practice-based training components. Thus, the cooperating schools must necessarily be chosen according to their proximity and accessibility to the ESE/IPP. From the group of schools that fulfil this condition mentors are recruited on the basis of personal relations and of the knowledge that the professors of the ESE/IPP, in charge of supervising practice, have their performance and motivation as trainers, rather than being based on settled principles and profiles.

Considering the responsibility of both institutions, and of the actors involved in the training process it was confirmed that:

- schools and the ESE/IPP lack knowledge on their educational projects;
- the managing boards of the schools are often unaware of the ESE training project, which is usually known only by the mentors;
- there was a total lack of joint reflection about the principles and purposes of the training, both from the actors more directly involved, and from the institutions they represented.

Difficulties impacting upon the development of the training project were identified as follows.

- A very limited number of actors were involved. From the schools, there were only the cooperating teachers. The team confirmed the lack of involvement in the process: (1) from the management boards, which in most cases did no more than tolerate this cooperation; (2) from the other teachers (and from the education community in general) of the cooperating schools; and (3) from the ESE teachers who are responsible for the other training components.
- In spite of the contracted arrangements the lack of organisation generated enormous difficulties for the actors most directly involved. (1) First, the mentor. Considering that this activity was seen as something exterior to the school, the conditions for the organisation and compatibility of schedules and the necessary facilities for the conducting of the reflection meetings at the appropriate time were never created. There are also no compensations foreseen, for example, concerning the reduction of teaching hours so that it would be possible for them to work together with the other partners involved in the training, nor any other sort of compensation (remuneration or any possibility of improvement in their careers). (2) Second, the students, namely their difficulties resulting from an overcharged schedule on their training curricula.

In considering the assessment of the training project, given the absence and/or ambiguousness of the process of defining the assessment criteria, most of the responsibility for assessing the performance of the future teachers during and at the end of their practice activity, and the assessment of the whole process, relies upon the ESE practice supervisors.

Some strategies were identified towards the desired cooperation, as follows.

- Assessment and re-elaboration of the ESE/IPP educational project.
- Selection of the cooperating schools, through a public contest among the basic education schools in Porto and the surrounding area with reference to the parameters of the cooperation, namely: (1) the profile of the cooperating teacher/trainer; (2) documentation to be presented by the applicant schools, particularly referring to their educational school project; and (3) resources made available by the ESE/IPP.
- Design of the practice project by a team of representatives of the ESE/IPP, including the students (future teachers), and members of all the schools selected.
- Launching of this process in due time (at the beginning of the second semester before the school year when the practice shall take place).

Unfortunately these strategies have not been implemented and we face today the same difficulties as before.

### The Conclusions of the Higher Education National Evaluation System: external evaluation committees' reports

The Higher Education National Evaluation System applied to both HEIs and courses brought some direct and reliable knowledge about the reality of teacher training in Portugal, namely concerning practice and mentoring, creating the possibility of bringing to light some research-based evidence through the review of the external evaluation committees' reports in charge of teacher training higher education courses and institutions.

In relation to nursery educators and the first and second cycle of basic education teacher training, one such study (Afonso & Canário, 2000), which considered 34 reports (nine public university departments and 12 public and 13 private polytechnic schools), demonstrates that the 'co-ordination of teachers' practice with other components, namely didactics and teaching methodologies is not always assured' and also that 'the choice of schools and mentors does not always follow a pre-defined set of criteria' (Afonso, 2002, p. 24). This study also stresses the 'insufficient scientific and pedagogical framework of cooperating schools and mentors' (p. 29).

A similar study concerning the third cycle of basic education and secondary education teacher training demonstrates an even more complex reality as HEIs develop a fragmented approach to the curriculum, thereby experiencing strong difficulties in the articulation of the so-called 'scientific area' with the 'educational area'. The first is seen as the 'real science', the second as the 'technical' one. In accordance with these principles, practice is nothing more than the level of 'application' (Canário, 2002). In one of the external evaluation reports underlying this research it is stated that:

> both in the case of the integrated initial teacher training courses and in the case of the 'educational option' of the Faculties of Humanities and Faculties of Science graduate courses, we find increasing difficulties – in some cases already insurmountable ones – to assure a satisfying functioning of practice. Most basic and secondary schools cannot receive any more teacher students ... It becomes therefore a necessity to disseminate the practice groups within a wide geographical area (some of them are placed in schools that are 150 miles away from the university) ... To all these difficulties we should add another one, which is the increasingly difficult recruitment of mentors having a minimum satisfactory professional expertise and experience. We can find the extreme situation of recruiting as a mentor someone who was a teacher student the year before. (Canário, 2002, p. 48)

### Continuous Teacher Training

From 1993 on, continuous teacher training (CTT) underwent considerable development in terms of both the legal framework and its effective implementation. It was poorly developed before that date as it was reduced to a few unsystematic activities sponsored by the Ministry of Education or the individual initiative of teachers (usually by attending formal graduate courses in order to obtain a master's degree or doctorate). A factor that very much contributed to the increase in CTT was the financial support provided by EU and national funding, making it completely free of charge for the trainees. At the same time continuous training is a condition for career advancement.

The legal framework for CTT established a balanced and adequate training system that succeeded in receiving a broad consensual approval on the part of all the educational interest groups. As the most positive aspects we should stress:

- the role acknowledged to schools and teachers in the assessment of their training needs and in the elaboration of the corresponding training plan strengthened through the creation of the associate schools' continuous training centres and the associate teachers' continuous training centres by the Ministry of Education, endowing those centres with the necessary budget and a self-governing structure;
- the broad scope of the acknowledged training institutions: HEIs (ITT institutions and also those more related to the science of education and sciences related to school subjects); the associate schools' continuous training centres as well as teacher centres; and on a supplementary basis the services of the Ministry of Education;
- a broad and adequate scope of the content, levels and modalities of the training programmes having in mind their adjustment to the needs of the Portuguese education system.

One difference from ITT is the control of training supply and quality, which, in this continuous teacher training system, is assigned to the Conselho Científico-Pedagógico da Formação Contínua de Professores (CCPFCP) (Scientific and Pedagogical Council for Continuous Teacher Training), an independent body with regard both to the Ministry of Education and to the training institutions and centres integrating one president and 12 members representative of the higher education training institutions as well as of the teaching staff. Although the Ministry of Education appoints them and financially supports the council, no ministry representative is included. The main tasks of this council are the accreditation of the training entities, of the trainers and of the training programmes together with the general evaluation of the whole CTT system.

Associate schools and teacher training centres were created all over the country immediately after the legislation was passed. In addition the offer of continuous training by HEIs soon developed in both quantity and diversity, showing that this policy was considered very positive by all stakeholders.

The activity reports published regularly by the council show some quantitative as well as qualitative data that are very useful for the understanding and evaluation of this process. In December 1997 accreditation had been awarded to 360 training entities (203 associate school centres for CTT, 56 associate teacher centres for CTT, 88 HEIs and 12 central administration bodies), 6628 training activities and 5101 trainers. In terms of the modalities of training we can identify a tendency to a higher degree of diversification. In the first years we find a more significant number of higher education single subjects and training modules, while more recently the number of training in context or school-based training activities like seminars, workshops and school-based projects has been increasing. The 3769 new training activities accredited during 1999 are distributed as follows: 2584 training courses (including training in specialised areas like school administration, special education, communitarian education, school inspection, pedagogical supervision and curriculum development), 131 training modules, 38 seminars, 580 workshops, 30 practicum-related activities, 137 projects and 269 circles of studies (CCPFCP, 1999). According to the last activity report of the council, the rate of training activities per training modality was 82.6% subject-centred and 17.4% school context-based in 1998 and 64.3% and 35.7%, respectively, in 2002 (CCPFCP, 2002). It cannot be concluded directly from these figures that there has been an increase in the importance of mentoring. However, when teachers do teamwork around common professional concerns and interests they adopt a reflective interactive attitude that also creates an opportunity for some kind of mentorship.

It can be concluded that CTT has been a successful domain of Portuguese educational policy regarding both the underlying principles and the conditions of its development according to a participatory approach which at the same time makes every CTT stakeholder more responsible and accountable. It is regrettable that it has been implemented so late. The sustainability of the CTT system is now the responsibility of, on an equal basis, teachers themselves, schools as teaching-learning organisations and higher education teacher training institutions.

### Mentoring: an open agenda

A new Education Act has recently been approved by the national Assembly of the Republic and is now waiting for presidential acceptance in order to be implemented. A new structure of the education system is to be established, namely the re-inclusion of the seventh, eighth and ninth form in the secondary education level (lower secondary), therefore establishing six years of basic education and six years of secondary education. Compulsory education is extended to 12 years for pupils entering school during 2005. There is not much difference in what concerns ITT. As mentioned before, the training principles set by the Education Act 1986 with the amendments of 1997 still in force reflect the state of the art and do not therefore need to change. The problem is its effective implementation. Considering that the induction year is already foreseen in the Portuguese legal framework, it is most probable that it will come into force so that the professional credential will be obtained only after that period:

> The relations between initial (pre-service) and in-service TE
> [teacher education] are a pressing contemporary dilemma for
> most countries. Induction periods and in-service activities
> have emerged as new orientations within TE. There is a

recognised need in many countries to integrate these three aspects of TE, e.g. in terms of life-long learning conceptions or models of continuous TE ... In particular the school-based component – teaching practice – seems at present to be in need of new orientations. It has to be kept in mind that this component is still very weak in many countries. This partly explains the emphasis put on induction programmes in some countries where such programmes accordingly are discussed in terms very similar to those used in countries where school-based components within ITE [initial teacher education] programmes are strong. (Thematic Network on Teacher Education in Europe, Sigma Report, 1999)

It is not clear, however, who is going to control induction: the HEIs? The Ministry of Education through its administrative and/or inspectorial structures together with schools? Or should it be done on a partnership basis between higher education initial training institutions, schools and the administrative authorities somehow like CTT? It is a fact that historically, mentoring only received support and recognition from the educational authorities when it was independent of HEIs. It is therefore conceivable that higher education initial training institutions, having lost their opportunity to develop such a partnership, do not have the legitimacy to claim it, and perhaps they will lose the control they had during two decades over initial teacher education and professionalisation.

### References

Afonso, N. (2002) *A Avaliação da Formação de Educadores de Infância e Professores dos 1º e 2º Ciclos do Ensino Básico in INAFOP: estudos sobre a situação da formação inicial de professores.* Porto: Porto Editora.

Arroteia, J. (1996) *O Ensino Superior em Portugal.* Aveiro: Universidade de Aveiro.

Buchberger, F., Campos, B.P., Kallos, D. & Stephenson, J. (2000) *Green Paper on Teacher Education in Europe: high quality teacher education for high quality education and training.* Umea: Thematic Network on Teacher Education in Europe Editorial Office.

Canário, R. (2002) Formação Inicial de Professores: que futuro(s)? in Instituto Nacional de Acreditação da Formação dos Professores (INAFOP) (Ed.) *Estudos Sobre a Situação da Formação Inicial de Professores.* Porto: Porto Editora.

Conselho Científico-Pedagógico da Formação Contínua (CCPFCP) (1999) *Relatório de Actividades.* Braga: CCPFCP.

Conselho Científico-Pedagógico da Formação Contínua (CCPFCP) (2002) *Relatório de Actividades.* Braga: CCPFCP.

Cunha, P. (1994) A Evolução do Ensino Particular e Cooperativo na Vigência do XI Governo Constitucional (1987-1991), in R. Carneiro (Ed.) *Ensino Livre: uma fronteira da hegemonia estatal.* Porto: ASA Ed.

Departamento de Programação e Gestão Financeira (DEPGEF) (1996) *Estatisticas da Educacio: 1992-1993.* Lisbon: Ministério da Educação/DEPGEF.

Thematic Network on Teacher Education in Europe (TNTEE) (1999) Synthesis Sigma Pilot Project: teacher education in Europe, evaluation and perspectives. Available at: http://tntee.umu.se/publications/publications.html

UNESCO (1995) *World Education Report 1995.* Oxford: UNESCO.

CHAPTER 4

---

# Continuing Professional Development for Leaders and Teachers: the English perspective

## KIT FIELD

### Key Players and their Role in Continuing Professional Development

Full appreciation of the arguments presented in this chapter demands a complete understanding of the roles and responsibilities of the 'key players' in the field of continuing professional development (CPD) in the teaching profession in England.

#### *Department for Education and Skills*

The Department for Education and Skills (DfES) is the government ministry which provides guidance and support for CPD. Its position in relation to CPD is summarised as follows:

> Continuing professional development (CPD) includes any
> activity that increases teachers' knowledge or understanding,
> and their effectiveness in schools. It can help raise teaching
> and learning standards and improve job satisfaction. CPD is for
> all teachers, at any stage of their career.
> (http://www.teachernet.gov.uk/professionaldevelopment/)

#### *National College for School Leadership*

The National College for School Leadership (NCSL) provides career-long learning and development opportunities and professional and practical support for England's existing and aspiring school leaders. The goal is to ensure that school leaders have the skills, recognition, capacity and ambition to transform the school education system into the best in the world (http://www.ncsl.org.uk/index.cfm?pageID=college-index).

### Teacher Training Agency

The purpose of the Teacher Training Agency (TTA) is to raise standards by attracting able and committed people to teaching and by improving the quality of training for teachers and the wider school workforce. The TTA is a government-sponsored independent body (http://www.tta.gov.uk).

### Higher Education Institutions

Higher education institutions (HEIs) include universities and colleges of higher education. These institutions have had responsibility for the academic accreditation of CPD, leading to master's degrees. Each institution works independently of others but is regulated by the TTA in terms of its work with teachers.

### General Teaching Council for England

The General Teaching Council for England's (GTC(E)'s) professional development advisory committee develops policy to enhance teachers' CPD. The CPD committee believes that a profession that is vibrant and forward-looking has CPD at its heart. The GTC represents teachers as a profession and advises the DfES on policy (http://www.gtce.org.uk/gtcinfo/cpdhome.asp).

### Local Education Authorities

Local education authorities (LEAs) as the employers of teachers within a local government authority have a responsibility for teachers' conditions of service and are also accountable for the levels of performance of the pupils in the local schools. The requirement to produce an education development plan demands that account is made of CPD and its impact in schools.

### Private Companies

Throughout the 1990s and early 2000s, private companies have entered the CPD market. Such companies are able to tender for national and regional projects as consultants and deliverers of CPD.

## Introduction

The launch of the national strategy for CPD (Department for Education and Employment [DfEE], 2001a) appeared to herald a new age in terms of teacher and school development, by galvanising a wide range of factors which have influenced the way teachers and school leaders learn and develop practice. The strategy was, on the whole, welcomed, and key principles upon which CPD was to be based (contained in the accompanying code of practice, DfEE (2001b)) provided a context and framework within which the profession should operate. Bolam (2001) indicated that these key publications provided the profession with fresh challenges and opportunities.

Bolam's (1986) analysis of CPD had shown that policy in this area had fallen into two discrete camps, which could be seen to be at either end of a continuum. Systems-led approaches are essentially managerialist, in that they are intended to secure the implementation of government, LEA and/or school policy. On the other hand, CPD to support the individual is designed to enhance personal motivation, job satisfaction and hence performance.

Both elements are still evident today. The context has become even more complex. There is inevitably a new political agenda; one which places 'choice' at the heart of education. Secondary schools are to be required to specialise, perceived effective schools will expand to accommodate more pupils and 'failing' schools will be closed down and replaced by 'city academies'.

The success of schools has been accredited to effective leadership (Sammons et al, 1995). Leadership development and training are very much aligned with school effectiveness. The NCSL is very much tasked with developing leaders who are able to 'raise standards'.

At the other end of Bolam's continuum are the individual teachers. The first of 10 key principles contained within the national strategy (DfEE, 2001a) is:

- teacher ownership and a shared commitment to, and responsibility for (by teachers and schools), development.

The emerging Teachers' Professional Learning Framework and the Teacher Learning Academy developed by the GTC(E) offers acknowledgement of personal professional development. Acknowledgement, recognition and advancement are readily available, thereby providing further motivation for teachers.

The TTA continues to fund HEIs for accredited professional development, now under the title of personal professional development (PPD). This enables teachers to earn credits towards master's-level qualifications and taught doctorates.

In these ways, and others, both ends of Bolam's (1986) continuum are catered for. The situation is, however, more complex. CPD is designed, also, to enhance the status and improve the profile and effectiveness of the profession as a whole. The GTC(E)'s Teaching and Learning Academy and the development by the DfES of a professional standards framework, a common electronic portfolio to plan and record teachers' professional development and career progress, all serve to provide a recognisable and distinctive career structure and routes for further progression.

The development of new approaches has been 'put out to tender' in the developing educational marketplace. Not only do new and existing national institutions (DfES, TTA, NCSL, GTC(E), LEAs, HEIs) have different roles to play, so do those who successfully bid for the projects. As a response to Richard Pring's radical view:

> The advisory bodies have been abolished; the Schools Council closed down, Her Majesty's Inspectorate as an independent critical voice emasculated; the counteracting influence of local education authorities enfeebled; the language of education impoverished; the curriculum imposed by politicians; the inevitably perennial deliberations over what is worth learning foreclosed. (Pring, 1996, p. 117)

It could be argued that new organisations, in the private sector, have adopted roles and responsibilities. CfBT, Nord Anglia, SERCO Learning and the more entrepreneurial HEIs have profited from the development opportunities. The place of the LEA as a provider of CPD has diminished, yet LEAs continue to play significant roles in shaping the CPD provision as a whole.

A key feature of the national CPD strategy (DfEE, 2001a) was the encouragement of teachers learning from and with each other. New forms of collaboration between teachers and schools have proliferated in recent years:

- beacon schools with outreach responsibilities;
- leadership incentive groups (LIGs);
- networked learning communities;
- Excellence in Cities;
- education action zones;
- advance skills teachers with outreach responsibilities;
- consultant leaders with outreach responsibilities.

Working and learning together is certainly a means by which professional development can serve to lift the morale of the profession (Puttman, 2001).

There are, then, a complex and interrelated set of goals for CPD: powerful 'new players', the development of new courses and apparently new approaches which seem to be simultaneously mutually supportive and yet also incompatible with each other. Within an ever-shifting political context, these propositions demonstrate the complexity, but also the opportunities available to teachers and leaders in an educational context. Figure 1 illustrates the extent to which the 'forces' overlap, yet at the same time create professional tensions.

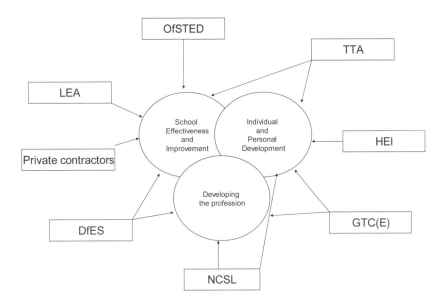

Figure 1. Forces and tensions associated with CPD in England.

The figure shows how the inner circles overlap, thereby indicating that *all* the *external* organisations influence *all* aspects of CPD – yet some more directly than others. The challenge brought about by the complexity is that each external organisation must maximise its impact on all aspects, without adversely affecting the influence of the other institutions.

### Defining CPD

CPD is still a new term. It evokes memories of the James Report (Department for Education and Science, 1972), which recommended periodic training and development for teachers, through sabbaticals and periods of professional and academic refreshment. It also links with individual and collective morale, self-esteem, status and professional control. Development relates to improvement, which brings to mind a process which involves exposure and access to ideas, reflection, implementation and evaluation. The impact of development is widespread, affecting the school and teachers themselves and learners.

It comes as no surprise that CPD can become a management tool. Close analysis of the terminology and associated concepts reveals the potential of CPD, and also its uses.

### (1) Continuing

Society is ever-changing. If one goal of education is to prepare young people today for the world of tomorrow, no teacher can rely on lessons learned yesterday. Teachers must engage in learning for practical reasons. The CPD strategy (DfEE, 2001a) mentions the need for pupils to develop an enthusiasm for lifelong learning, as it is seen to be a key to success in adult life. Such an enthusiasm is more likely to develop if young people see their teachers modelling such practices.

O'Brien & MacBeath (1999, p. 73) comment:

> Teacher lifelong learning in the form of continuing
> professional development (CPD) is increasingly regarded as an
> important means of contributing to the creation of more
> effective schools, and as integral to learning organisations.

To follow this argument through to its logical conclusion: lifelong learning leads to the development of a learning organisation, which continuously and collectively re-evaluates its purposes and seeks ways to develop the most effective and efficient ways of reaching its goals. Improvement is continuous if learning is ongoing.

Continuous and continuing learning is not problematic. The core 'business' of a school is teaching and learning. All teachers therefore have access to teaching and learning situations all day, prompting Estelle Morris (2001) to assert that teachers learn best from teachers. This does suggest the need for contact, communication and regular access to other teachers. Putnam & Borko (2000) condemn the traditional view that teachers should 'find their own style' in that it encourages a paradigm of privacy. For them, the development of a community of learners leads to the establishment of a common theory and language, and opportunities to challenge assumptions. 'Continuing Professional Development relies on regular interaction with colleagues' (Putnam & Borko, 2000, p. 24).

### (2) Professional

The word 'professional' is problematic. Certainly Estelle Morris uses the term to draw approval for the strategy from teachers: '[CPD] ... is part of the reprofessionalisation of what teachers should do, shout as loudly as we possibly can that, yes, we demand a lot of teachers' (Morris, 2001).

Professionalising teachers means for some (e.g. Whitty, 2000) providing independence and self-governance. Within the strategy, some allowance is made, in that teachers are encouraged to take responsibility for professional development, as, it is claimed, it is increasingly a requirement in other professions. This does not go as far as Whitty (2000) would want – to have, as a profession, a mandate to act on behalf of the state. Education is, and will continue to be, subject to and regulated by market forces and subject to supervision by the government.

To a degree, some features of a profession are in place:

- teacher skills are based on theoretical knowledge;
- education in the skills is certified by examination;
- there is a code of conduct (DfEE, 2001b) oriented towards the public good;
- a new professional organisation (GTC) enjoys some power and influence (after Whitty, 2000).

The impact of the above is difficult to measure. Puttman (2001) argues that the existence of the GTC provides some self-regulation, and that the implementation of the CPD strategy will lead to 'thought leadership'.

Day's (1999) analysis, drawing on Hoyle's (1980) definitions of professionalism and professionality, is less positive. Characteristics of the 'restricted professional' are applicable. Action is intuitive, and learning is derived from the work base. Experience rather than theory is used to justify action. Teachers are not encouraged by the CPD strategy to become 'extended professionals', that is to locate practice in a broader political and social context. The extent to which teaching is 'value-led' is also questionable. The 'values' are imposed; present in the TTA's latest set of standards for qualified teacher status. The values have not emerged from the profession itself.

The CPD strategy is moving towards the professionalisation of teachers. It is contributing towards the professionality of teacher behaviour and practice, but as yet stops short of providing the decision- and policy-making powers traditionally associated with professions.

### (3) Development

Field & Philpott (2000) comment on the modes of engaging with teaching and learning in the context of initial teacher education. They identify activities which provide trainee teachers with learning opportunities, and the mentoring and coaching activities which shape actual practice. In the context of CPD, this involves learning, and changing (rather than shaping) practice. Development, or improvement of practice, is then further enhanced by evaluation. Development, then, consists of two distinct phases: (1) learning activities and processes; and (2) application and evaluation.

There is no option to withdraw from development. All teachers do model learning for their pupils, whether they choose to do so or not. Pupils experience teacher development first-hand. With pupil learning as the core business of schools, it makes sense to assert that teachers must model lifelong learning.

For motivational proposes, teachers, as learners, must recognise the fruits of their labour. Evaluation enhances learning and development. OfSTED inspections of CPD provision, and access to funding through application to the TTA, both demand the demonstration of measurable impact on pupil learning. As Rhodes & Houghton-Hill (2000) confirm, the requirement to demonstrate linkage between professional learning of teachers and classroom improvement is firmly established. It is this linkage which served to convert professional learning into professional development.

## CPD as a Means of Supporting School Development

School development can be divided into three discrete categories.

### (1) School Effectiveness

School effectiveness can be equated with 'raising standards'. Rhodes & Houghton-Hill (2000) identified one key goal of CPD: to help teachers deal with the changes demanded by policy and legislation. Such policies and legislation are informed by research into school effectiveness, which, in essence, is measured by performance data and which results in the setting of performance-related targets. Hammersley (1997, p. 215) warns: 'Put into practice an exclusive focus on effectiveness leads to an over-emphasis on those outcomes that can be measured (at the expense of other educational goals)'.

Pollard (2002) recognises CPD to be a core element of school effectiveness. Through performance, management procedures, individual teachers' development activities, subject departments' plans and school development plans, priorities are designed to meet defined and measurable performance targets.

Hargreaves's (1996) introduction of the concept of evidence-based practice has, to an extent, been hijacked by the school effectiveness movement. The publication of performance tables, the development of 'value-added measures' and the resultant culture of target setting are all embedding school effectiveness in the day-to-day practice of education professionals. Indeed, the ability to understand and use assessment data is contained within the national standards for teachers at all stages of their career. Teachers aspiring to 'threshold' status and also to advanced skills teacher status are required to demonstrate effective teaching and learning through the presentation of statistical data. This presentation, it is assumed, proves a causal link between teaching and improved pupil performance. OfSTED inspections, enquiries and surveys have all focused sharply on the impact of accredited CPD. There is no doubt that CPD has become one means of supporting school effectiveness.

### (2) School Improvement

School improvement does not equate with increased school effectiveness. School improvement is concerned with capacity building and the empowerment of all teachers. Frost et al (2000) argue positively that real improvement and development are dependent upon teacher agency and a positive and supportive school culture. There is, as Moon (2000) notes, a direct relationship between teachers' morale and self-esteem and school improvement. Indeed, the national CPD strategy does place 'professional development at the heart of school improvement' (Morris, 2001).

Stoll & Fink (1996) have demonstrated the interrelationship between school effectiveness and school improvement. Figure 2 shows how a school may be any combination of effective and improving.

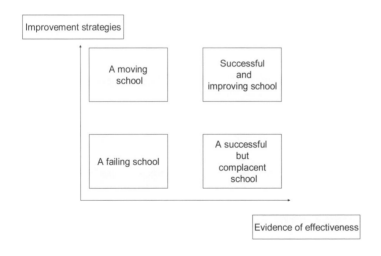

Figure 2. How a school may be any combination of effective
and improving. Adapted from Stoll & Fink (1996).

Such a model demonstrates the advantages of an integrated approach to CPD. The request by the DfES that HEIs provide master's-level accreditation for teachers engaging in the implementation of the Key Stage 3 strategy exemplifies this more integrative approach. The Key Stage 3 strategy is concerned primarily with raising standards (school effectiveness), and master's-level study implies an element of challenge, criticality and the integration of theoretical perspectives and practice. Similarly, the NCSL has secured agreements with HEIs to provide accreditation opportunities for leaders completing the Leading from the Middle course, the National Professional Qualification for Headteachers and the Leadership for Serving Headteachers (LPSH). The GTC(E) is also engaging with HEIs, through the Universities' Commission for Education and Training (UCET) CPD committee, to align progression through the Learning and Teaching Academy with master's- and doctorate-level credits.

This greater respect for individual teachers' judgements and perspectives is evidence of a recognition of the school improvement role CPD can play. As Eraut (1994) points out, teachers need to be able to:

- access and acquire information;
- be skilled to apply a full range of competencies;
- have the deliberative skills and processes to enable informed decision making;
- provide information and ideas to others;
- be intellectually able to generalise and make meaningful conclusions.

Accredited CPD enhances CPD for school effectiveness purposes, building a capacity for school improvement.

### (3) School Transformation

School transformation is best summed up by Bennis & Biederman's (1997) popular maxim: it is not about 'doing things better, but doing better things'.

Transformational leadership is actively encouraged and promoted by the NCSL, throughout its raft of leadership training programmes. Participants are presented with tasks of 'visioning' and 'development planning' in order to realise their visions. Monitoring, evaluation and review are dependent upon the (learnt) skills of analysing and presenting school effectiveness data.

For teachers, although Estelle Morris (2001) recognised the national literacy and numeracy strategies to be 'essentially [a] professional development programme for teachers', the encouragement of classroom enquiry and research has been explicit. The approach was funded initially through the Best Practice Research Scholarship scheme, professional bursaries for teachers in their fourth and fifth year of teaching and, more recently, through the GTC's publication of teachers' research of the month, and the NCSL finding of research associates and the publication of their outcomes on their website. The (re)introduction of education for creativity evident in DfES publications such as

*Excellence and Enjoyment* (DfES, 2004) and the Leading Edge Seminar Series (NCSL) gives greater authority to teachers and schools shaping the future. Sponsorship of Bentley's (2004) research and projections into the future of schooling and education similarly indicates the acceptance of a growing school transformation movement.

## CPD as a Means of Supporting the Individual

School leaders and teachers are employed in the learning industry. It therefore follows that they should be engaged in learning as part of their working lives.

> Learners will inherit the earth. Knowers will find they inhabit
> a world which no longer exists.

Motivation and morale are key to successful professional performance. CPD must focus on individual needs and aspirations. Hopkins's (2002) *Think Tank Report to the Governing Council* of the NCSL recommended that the 'route map' for school leaders should take account of principles of adult learning – one being that (particularly) adult learners have preferred learning styles, and that the full range of such styles should be reflected in NCSL provision. Collarbone's (2001) review of the LPSH urged recognition that individual characteristics determined 25% of the effectiveness of a leader. She recommended a continued focus on how individuals, in practice, can apply knowledge, understanding, skills and attributes to the development of a school. Collarbone (2001) confirmed that 'personal effectiveness' aspects of the programme are more effective than the 'organisational effectiveness' aspects.

The criteria for the TTA-funded PPD programme (the funding of master's-level accredited CPD) contain the requirement that providers structure programmes around individual participant needs. HEIs seeking funding must demonstrate how individual needs analyses/self-audits inform the content of programmes and the learning experiences contained within programmes. Accreditation is personal in that awards are made to individuals, not groups, and HEIs are required through Quality Assurance Agency (QAA) guidelines to provide pastoral support and personal academic guidance. The Church Colleges and University CPD Network (2002) is very explicit about the focus on the individual. In spelling out the values underpinning provision, it has included an emphasis on:

- personhood;
- wholeness;
- growth;
- identity and self-esteem.

71

The DfES, NCSL and GTC(E) have all developed frameworks to support teachers in the planning of their own career progression.

Newly qualified teachers are required to complete a career entry and development profile, and to identify personal targets for improvement. The Professional Standards Framework enables teachers to relate their current standard of performance to a role to which they aspire. A comparison of standards in this way facilitates personal action planning with particular career ambitions in mind. The soon to be published 'e-portfolio' further assists individual teachers to link their plans to case studies and examples of related professional development, thereby offering examples of models of professional development appropriate to the individual teachers' needs and aspirations.

The GTC(E)'s Learning and Teaching Academy provides an alternative stance. In recognition of teachers' current and future contributions in the role they occupy, rather than one they aspire to, a 'framework of recognition' has been developed. Teachers may be associates, members, associate fellows or fellows of the academy.

Such labels must be 'earned' though successful completion of projects designed to improve pupils' learning experiences. Awards are not given in recognition of current levels of performance, but for development and capacity building – feeding the transformation agenda. This framework, particularly when coupled with academic accreditation through association with HEIs, embodies key educational goals relevant to the individual in a professional context:

- a predilection for lifelong learning;
- keeping pace with societal and technological change;
- school development depends on teacher development;
- content and pedagogy are not separable.

If, as Day (1999) asserts, individual teachers are a school's greatest asset, it is essential that CPD addresses teachers' personal, individual and professional needs and wants.

### CPD as a Means of Developing the Profession

The requirement that funding will be made available if CPD is intended to influence the pupil learning experience in a positive way, and that the evidence to support such a claim must be presented, is becoming known as 'impact funding'.

For some, impact funding is perceived as a means of imposing a way of working, and less as a means of offering personal and professional development opportunities. Whitty (2000) sees the measures as a means of specifying outputs, and a way of defining the content of what teachers should do. This can lead to a feeling of deprofessionalisation, and a restriction of autonomy and self-direction. By its own admission (DfEE,

2001a), the national framework of teacher standards is intended to show teachers what they can aspire to, and to help monitor progress and to plan CPD. The standards for teachers at all stages of their career provide clarity in terms of job specifications and expectations, but at the same time can reduce the sense of teachers' professional judgement (Whitty, 2000). Blandford (2000, p. 66) lists the purposes of the standards:

> – to establish clear and explicit expectations of teachers
> – to help set targets for professional development and career progression
> – to help to focus and improve training and staff development at national, local and school levels
> – to ensure that the focus at every point is on improving pupil achievement
> – to recognise the expertise required of effective headteachers and teachers in school.

However, CDP is also, Estelle Morris (2001) states, a means of acknowledging what teachers have to do, and of recognising their commitment to the task. The collective responsibility of the profession, and the individual's commitment to teaching and learning, are ongoing learning and development experiences. Teachers need to be helped to 'accommodate new initiatives and requirements' (Pollard, 2002, p. 404), but also need to drive the process themselves. Interpretation of, and response to, such initiatives require time, reflection, evaluation and professional sharing. Working as a professional community is recognised to be essential (DfEE, 2001a). Professional communities must, therefore, extend beyond the confines of a single school. Their role is to identify and to address concerns which emanate from professional practice. A collective response is, therefore, seen to be a move towards a *professional* engagement.

According to the DfEE (2001a), successful professional development involves:

- a focus upon specific teaching and learning problems;
- opportunities for teachers to reflect on what they know and do already;
- opportunities for teachers to understand the rationale behind new ideas and approaches; to see theory demonstrated in practice; to be exposed to new expertise;
- sustained opportunities to experiment with new ideas and approaches, so that teachers can work out their implications for their own subject, pupils, school and community;
- opportunities for teachers to put their own interpretation on new strategies and ideas to work, building on their existing knowledge and skills;

- coaching and feedback on their professional practice over a period of weeks and months. This is a particularly important element, and can be decisive in determining whether changes in practice survive.

Too often CPD has been either systems-led (Bolam, 1986) or individually focused. Bolam (2001) argues a need for the pendulum to swing back in favour of the individual. However, too great an emphasis on the individual can be counter-productive. The development and changing of practice remain personal and fail to add to a community's collective body of knowledge if they are not externalised. Moon (2000) argues that dissemination of PPD is essential, if such developments are to add to teachers' repertoires and understanding of theory. Deep learning must stand the test of professional scrutiny and evaluation. Working in collaboration through networked learning communities, LIGs and excellence clusters, for example, supports *externalisation.* Dissemination through the publication of academic journal articles has been seen to be inaccessible to teachers. The GTC's teachers' research of the month and NCSL web-based research associate reports represent deliberate attempts to make good and best practice available to a wide range of interested professionals.

If inward-looking views are not made explicit and 'put to the test' there is a risk of developing 'learning disabilities' (MacBeath & Mortimore, 2001). CPD does need to involve the examination and scrutiny of practice and personal theory if such 'disabilities' are to be overcome:

- teachers projecting their own deficiencies on children or their communities;
- teachers clinging to past practices;
- defences built up against threatening messages from outside;
- fear of failure;
- seeing change as someone else's job;
- hostile relationships which annoy staff;
- seeking safety in numbers (a ring-fenced mentality).

CPD intended to develop the profession can be constrained by the outcomes intended by the government. Organisers of CPD are therefore both constrained and enabled by government regulations and guidelines. Bolam (2001, p. 272) explains that:

> The essence of professional development for educators must surely involve the learning of an independent, evidence informed and constructively critical approach to practice within a public framework of professional values and accountability, which are also open to critical scrutiny.

Professionalism, we have seen, involves the liberation of teachers from central control, but public accountability demands justification for action taken and the measurement of success. Hargreaves (1996) and Hammersley (1997) both recognise research and the active use of evidence by teachers as the way forward. Research, Hammersley (1997) argues, allows the illumination of aspects of teaching and learning which are below the normal level of consciousness, and Hargreaves's (1996) advocation of an evidence-based profession involves converting information needs into answerable questions, research to generate evidence to answer the questions, a critique of the validity and reliability of the evidence, the application of justifiable theories and the measurement and evaluation of performance. In these ways teachers seize control of development and are able to base development work on real practice.

It is, perhaps, therefore, evidence-based practice and the engagement of education professionals in the uncovering and generation of evidence and data, as well as the requirement to respond to relevant data, that lead to the empowerment of the profession as a whole. Stenhouse's (1975) dream of the teacher as a researcher, yet within a clear framework of accountability, is perhaps an answer. As HEIs encourage action research as a way of effecting change, and a critical narrative/journal (as is being discussed at the UCET) as the means of recording and disseminating real experiences, teachers do begin to establish an evidence base. Through collaboration with other agencies (TTA, DfES, GTC, NCSL) the profession will enjoy the opportunity of sharing and disseminating the process and outcomes of effective CPD.

### Conclusion

CPD for teachers and school leaders is undergoing considerable change – indeed, a paradigm shift. There are competing forces and a proliferation of 'frameworks' from key players, which create tensions. Organisers of CPD have to balance the intended outcomes, yet are beginning to recognise how one approach can actually enhance another. As relatively new institutions establish their roles in relation to each other and to more traditional institutions, a sense of integration and complementarity is emerging. A teacher can undertake CPD for her own personal reasons and benefit, yet simultaneously contribute to school development and to the status of the profession as a whole. The three sides to CPD are not mutually incompatible. The challenge is, of course, to make personal, institutional and professional goals compatible and transferable, thereby closing the gap between the 'professional' and the 'academic'. It is through a holistic approach that the impact of CPD will become evident. We await, in eager anticipation, the national CPD strategy of 2005.

## References

Bennis, W. & Biederman, P.W. (1997) *Learning to Lead.* London: Nicholas Brearley.

Bentley, T. (2004) ITE Futures. Available at: http://itefutures.tta.gov.uk

Blandford, S. (2000) *Managing Professional Development in Schools.* London: Routledge.

Bolam, R. (1986) Conceptually In-service, in D. Hopkins (Ed.) *In-service Training and Educational Development: an institutional survey.* London: Croom Helm.

Bolam, R. (2001) Challenges and Opportunities for CPD. Inaugural presidential address to the International Professional Development Association. October, Birmingham.

Church Colleges and University CPD Network (2002) Vision and Values for Church Colleges' and University Provision (unpublished).

Collarbone, P. (2001) *Leadership Programme for Serving Headteachers.* Nottingham: National College for School Leadership.

Day, C. (1999) *Developing Teachers: the challenges of lifelong learning.* London: Falmer Press.

Department for Education and Employment (DfEE) (2001a) *Learning and Teaching: a strategy for professional development.* London: DfEE.

DfEE (2001b) *Good Value CPD: a code of practice for providers of professional development for teachers.* London: DfEE.

Department for Education and Skills (DfES) (2004) *Excellence and Enjoyment.* London: DfES.

Department for Education and Science (1972) *The James Report – teacher education and training.* London: HMSO.

Eraut, M. (1994) *Developing Professional Knowledge and Competence.* London: Falmer Press.

Field, K. & Philpott, C. (2000) The Impact of Hosting Student Teachers on School Effectiveness and School Improvement, *Journal of In-service Education,* 26(1), pp. 115-138.

Frost, D., Durrant, J., Head, M. & Holden, G. (2000) *Teacher-led School Improvement.* London: RoutledgeFalmer.

Hammersley, M. (1997) Educational Research and Teaching: a response to David Hargreaves's TTA lecture, *British Educational Research Journal,* 25(2), reprinted in J. Moon, J. Butcher & E. Bird (Eds) (2000) *Leading Professional Development in Education,* pp. 211-223. London: RoutledgeFalmer & Open University.

Hargreaves, D.H. (1996) Teaching as a Research-based Profession: possibilities and prospects, TTA annual lecture 1996, reprinted in J. Moon, J. Butcher & E. Bird (Eds) (2000) *Leading Professional Development in Education,* pp. 200-210. London: RoutledgeFalmer & Open University.

Hopkins, D. (2002) *Think Tank Report to the Governing Council.* Nottingham: National College for School Leadership.

Hoyle, E. (1980) Professionalization and De-professionalization in Education, in E. Hoyle & J. Megarny (Eds) *World Yearbook of Education 1980: the professional development of teachers.* London: Kogan Page.

MacBeath, J. & Mortimore, P. (Eds) (2001) *Improving School Effectiveness.* Buckingham: Open University Press.

Moon, B. (2000) The Changing Agenda for Professional Development in Education, in J. Moon, J. Butcher & E. Bird (Eds) (2000) *Leading Professional Development in Education*, pp. 3-10. London: RoutledgeFalmer & Open University.

Morris, E. (2001) Keynote speech at the DfEE launch of the national strategy for CPD, 1 March.

O'Brien, J. & MacBeath, J. (1999) Co-ordinating Staff Development: the training and development of staff development coordinators, *Journal of In-service Education*, 25(1), pp. 69-84.

Pollard, A. (2002) *Reflective Teaching: effective and evidence – informed professional practice.* London: Continuum.

Pring, R. (1996) Values and Education Policy, in J.M. Halstead & M.J. Taylor (Eds) *Values in Education and Education in Values,* pp. 104-118. London: Falmer Press.

Puttman, D. (2001) Closing address at the DfEE launch of the national strategy for CPD, 1 March.

Putnam, R.T. & Borko, H. (2000) What do New Views of Knowledge and Thinking Have to Say about Research on Teacher Learning, *Educational Researcher,* 29(1), reprinted in J. Moon, J. Butcher & E. Bird (Eds) (2000) *Leading Professional Development in Education*, pp. 11-29. London: RoutledgeFalmer & Open University.

Rhodes, C. & Houghton-Hill, S. (2000) The Linkage of Continuing Professional Development and the Classroom Experience of Pupils: barriers perceived by senior managers in some secondary schools, *Journal of In-service Education*, 26(3), pp. 423-436.

Sammons, P., Hillman, J. & Mortimore, P. (1995) *Key Characteristics of Effective Schools: a review of school-effectiveness research.* London: Ofsted.

Stenhouse, L. (1975) *An Introduction to Curriculum Research and Development.* London: Heinemann.

Stoll, L. & Fink, D. (1996) *Changing Our Schools.* Buckingham: Open University Press.

Whitty, G. (2000) Teacher Professionalism in New Times, *Journal of In-service Education*, 26(2), pp. 281-296.

CHAPTER 5

---

# Continuing Professional Development for Leaders and Teachers: an Italian response

## FRANCESCA BROTTO

> We are only in the initial stages of an authentic awareness of professional learning as a place of social change. (Dutto, 2000, p. 37)

In November 2002, roughly 75% of Italy's tenured and supply teachers were over 40 years of age (Ministero dell'Istruzione, dell'Universita' e della Ricerca [MIUR], 2003). If we consider the mere fact that only starting in the 1999-2000 school year did it become mandatory to recruit secondary schoolteachers for permanent status on the basis of something more than a simple subject degree, and only in recent years have university degrees in education been available and required of would-be primary and pre-primary teachers, it is safe to affirm that there has been ample scope for professional development in Italian schools. Indeed, a pedagogical-track diploma from an upper secondary school (International Standard Classification of Education – ISCED 3) was all that was prescribed for pre-primary and primary teaching until a short while ago.

There has been just as much scope for the professional development of Italian school heads, who have seen their roles undergo radical change in the wake of the devolved self-management brought into Italian schools in September 2000.

Thus, well into the 1990s, in-service training was meant to cover for the profound weakness, inadequacy and anachronism of Italian pre-service training (Gattullo,1990). At the same time, it had to grapple with its own inherent weakness, arising from what it was expected to achieve, set against the lack of a quality control culture in the field (Neri, 2004) and the equally anachronistic means of staff development much of it employed (mainly talks, with little resort to more interactive, 'hands-on' professional development models (Cerini, 2000)).

In the late 1990s, new visions of what schools are about ushered in the concept of continuing professional development (CPD), seen not only as 'a means of individual improvement, but as an opportunity for organizational development' (Imperato, 2004, p. 88). However, although recent years have seen the substantial growth of non-linear, constructivist forms of professional learning in the country, the term itself has not actively entered the vocabulary of education policy makers and practitioners. Older terms such as *aggiornamento* and *formazione* seem to prevail, with the conflicting underpinning attitudes of things being 'done to' or 'done by' the interested parties (teachers and school principals) also marking a contrast in the country's dominant political cultures. At the heart of the issue is what Frost et al (2000, p. 11) describe as the power of 'agency', derived from Giddens (1984), meaning 'the human capacity to "make a difference" through the application of bottom-up power to change the structures which constrain and determine our actions'.

Notwithstanding, the massive e-learning professional development efforts, bordering on what Biondi (2003) terms 'x-learning', undertaken in the last five years by the Istituto Nazionale di Documentazione per l'Innovazione e la Ricerca Educativa (INDIRE) (National Educational Research Institute) in Florence with hundreds of thousands of Italian teachers and school heads, constitute one of the 'most advanced models of an integrated learning environment in Europe' (quotation from: www.indire.it). Moreover, important innovation in the tracking and qualitative 'valorisation' of professional learning, such as the Emilia-Romagna Education Authority's research and pilot project with teacher portfolios (Associazione Italiana Maestri Cattolici [AIMC] et al, 2004), can only extend our understanding of what CPD or, as Stoll et al (2003) prefer, continuous professional learning (CPL) might entail.

### Challenges for CPD from the
### Initial Training and Recruitment System

Tenured Italian teachers have civil servant status and are employed by the state, rather than by school boards or individual schools, as is common in many English-speaking countries. Until 1999, they had either been recruited through centralised *concorsi* (competitive examinations), requiring no previous specific professional training for the aspiring teachers, or had entered the profession on a stable basis by decree (*ope legis*), after what were usually many years of unsteady supply teaching. In both cases, after a probationary year in a provisional teaching position and a 40-hour course centred mainly on teaching methodology and some school law, teachers were *abilitati* or 'qualified' to teach on a permanent basis, once the school's internal *comitato di valutazione* (evaluation committee) had formally appraised their 'suitability' for the profession.

An obligatory subject degree with a follow-up two-year professional training period at university for all aspiring secondary teachers and a degree in (pre-) primary education for (pre-) primary teachers have since then been put in place as prerequisites for the *concorsi*. However, at the same time, the long list of 40-something-year-old practitioners still making a precarious living out of fill-in teaching continues to bear witness to the fact that the vast majority of us have learnt and trained directly *on the job* and *in the job*.

Many acting school heads are also in the parallel position of having entered the role with no specific preparation, but with an age difference compared with their teacher counterparts, as they tend to be in their 50s and 60s. Until the two very recent *ad hoc* 160-hour in-service training courses, followed by public examinations, were devised, destined to turn acting heads with three years' experience into 'school managers', well over a third of the schools in the country were being run by unqualified heads. These measures have lessened the shortage, which remains acute, in that other *dirigenti scolastici*, as they are called, are due to retire very soon.

There is, however, no teacher shortage as yet in the country, and in recent years the government has attempted to reduce the teaching population by not replacing retiring practitioners or by increasing teaching load. The salaries of Italian teachers, which are lower than the Organisation for Economic Co-operation and Development (OECD) mean, are 'the reverse side of years of non-selective recruitment policies that have inflated the teaching force' (Brotto, 2003) to a 1:10.3 teacher:pupil ratio in secondary education and 1:11 in primary education, as compared to the OECD country mean of 1:14.3 and 1:17.7 (OECD, 2002). Although all sorts of 'refresher' courses (but what is there to 'refresh' if one is lacking basic training?) have been made available to practitioners – whatever their status – in these last two decades, some crucial questions remain. To what extent have teachers actually been able to develop to their utmost as professionals *through and with the job*? To what extent do Italian practitioners perceive their job as *continually developing* and see themselves as *needing development*? Do they perceive the need to actively engage in and drive this development?

Similarly, for school heads, how do you turn a *preside* (qualified head of a secondary school in the pre-autonomy period) or a *direttore* (qualified head of a primary or pre-primary school before school autonomy) into a *dirigente scolastico*, a new status for Italian school heads as of September 2000, implying something akin to 'executive managers with corresponding tasks and areas of authorities' (Huber & Schratz, 2004, p. 211)? They come from the teaching profession – with the training problems briefly outlined above – and, in the past, had basically needed to be versed in school law and centrally defined administrative procedures in order to be appointed as heads, usually by competing in *concorsi*. A 300-hour training course was organised in 2000-01 to turn them into qualified, liable and accountable 'executive managers' (the school's legal representative, with responsibility for human resources, maintaining the school buildings and managing its finances) of autonomous schools. Has that done the job? And how does one implant the roots of CPD as a proactive leadership trait rather than professional development as a reactive management mind frame in the initial training process for new *dirigenti scolastici* in the future?

### Challenges for CPD from a Shifting Conceptual Framework

State directives related to the training and development of school staff and administrative personnel, together with the national work contracts of the last decade, do not offer a clear and consistent use of terms and mirror the contrasts of differing political agendas.

The *aggiornamento* (literally, 'updating' or 'refreshing') of the 1980s and early 1990s was conceived as both a 'duty' and a 'right' of teachers and heads and was essentially 'delivered' in top-down lecture-style settings. Much of the key in-service training designed to implement the major school reforms of these decades was planned in this way, and intended as a means to drive these reforms, promote school effectiveness and improve the quality of education, however much it was 'done to' the people involved. Indeed, these 'development' initiatives perhaps 'underestimated the identities, the vocational tendencies and the underlying competencies of the participants, by privileging uniform professional models' (Spinosi, 2004, p. 351). A distinction between 'in-service lessons' (*didattica in servizio*), aiming towards 'collective training', and 'professional development' meaning 'involvement in permanent and purposeful activities' for school people (Marczely, 1999) was yet to be made.

However, once the concept of *formazione* (in some respects meaning 'training' and in others similar to the German concept of *bildung*) started to make headway in school legislation in the late 1990s, one would have expected *formazione* to supplant *aggiornamento,* in that it was recognised, especially as *formazione continua* ('continuing education'), to be 'the fundamental strategic lever for professional development and ... for the support needed to implement change' (Contratto Collettivo Nazionale di Lavoro [CCNL], 1999). Nevertheless, the two terms seem to float together in interchangeable or complementary ways in later contract regulations (Contratto Collettivo Nazionale Integrativo [CCNI], 2001), while more recently *autoaggiornamento* (literally, 'self-directed updating') is proposed 'to support the professional development needs of teachers regarding subject content, [together with] methodological, teaching, organizational and research skills, and relationship management' (Direttiva Ministeriale 70, 2002). This adds to the laborious attempts at distinction among *formazione iniziale* (pre-service training), *formazione in ingresso* (training at the onset of a career or induction), *formazione permanente* ('continuing education') and *formazione in servizio* (in-service training) in other normative documents (Direttiva Ministeriale 74, 2002 and the Education Reform Law Legge 53, 2003).

Oddly enough, one might think, while the first state directive (Direttiva Ministeriale 226, 1998), aiming to set yearly professional development priorities in Italy coupled with funding guidelines for national and local initiatives, makes the breakthrough statement that 'a CPD perspective is to be adopted' (article 4) in the *formazione* and *aggiornamento* of school staff, this same outlook disappears in the more recent political agenda. The measures taken especially in the three years from 1998 to 2000 reach out towards an Italian conceptualisation of CPD and mark a radical rethinking of the in-service training process on the steering level. This signals a move away from the *ad hoc* and *una tantum* approaches used in implementing earlier school reforms. The head of what was then the Coordinamento per la Formazione degli Insegnanti (Teacher Development Coordinating Body) (since taken over by a General Directorate in the Ministry of Education and Research), Mario Dutto (2000, p. 33), speaks of the need to 'give up yesterday's terms – *aggiornamento, formazione in servizio*, etc. – in favour of the more pertinent and comprehensive concepts of *sviluppo professionale continuo* ['CPD'] and of *apprendimento professionale* ['professional learning']'. He lists a whole array of integrated ways (for example short courses and work placements) in which teachers may engage in formal and non-formal learning processes to 'build and rebuild' their skills and aptitudes. He echoes Directive 210 (1999), a milestone in Italian professional development policy, in calling for greater collaboration and partnership amongst schools and the universe of education research bodies, headteacher and teacher professional associations, higher education institutions (HEIs) and other accredited professional development agencies on the scene, so as to make the best use of the opportunities available. The directive also instituted the now-defunct Osservatorio di Orientamento e Monitoraggio (PD Steering and Monitoring Body), whose main function was to identify professional development needs, monitor professional development initiatives on the regional level and assess their impact.

The visionary scenario of schools as CPD workshops and places of CPL inspired the legislators who designed Italian school autonomy to include not only the teaching and organisational management side but also the pursuit of 'research, development and experimentation' (article 6, Decreto del Presidente della Repubblica [DPR] 275, 1999). Article 7 of the same decree points to how school networks and liasing with the wider environment may become the natural setting for such a scenario.

However, in contrast to such a vision there are at least two challenges characterising the nitty-gritty reality of schools and the policy which frames their practice. On the one hand, there is still insufficiently widespread perception of CPD/CPL as 'an ordinary activity that is part of the daily and habitual practice' (Neri, 2004, p. 21) of being a teacher, or even a school leader. In the last two years, a series of workshops with Italian teacher leaders (*funzione-obiettivo* teachers, now called *funzioni strumentali al Piano dell'Offerta Formativa*) dedicated to a reflection on the meaning and use of professional time have revealed how even many of these teachers fail to recognise activities such as informal professional dialogue and exchange (whether at the workplace or in online forums), contributions to education newsletters and journals or individual reflection on knowledge and practice as *professional time* (Brotto, 2004). What is more significant is that for still too many school heads, staff development seems to be someone else's business, as they 'phone up' the experts to give a talk to their teachers and they then disappear altogether in the process (Scurati, 2003). This is not because they have decided that a low-key non-interfering profile is the most suitable in this case, allowing teachers to experience external support without pressure, but rather it is the *aggiornamento* paradigm of ineffective, non-mutual and often passive involvement. This says a lot also in relation to how these principals might perceive their own professional development as something not to be undertaken with their teachers in the school environment. In leadership conferences geared to both a teacher and a principal audience, it is not uncommon to hear *dirigenti scolastici* query: 'What are the teachers doing here?'

Nonetheless, things are not as bad as they might seem.

The current policy picture poses another challenge to the 'research, development and experimentation' role of schools, as asserted in the 1999 Regolamento sull'Autonomia Scolastica recalled above (DPR 275). In 2002, when the Education Reform Act (Legge 59, 2003) was still a bill in Parliament, the Consiglio Nazionale della Pubblica Istruzione (CNPI) (National Educational Council), a national body of experts appointed to advise Parliament on education policy, was called upon to express its mandatory opinion on various matters in the document. Its members informed the Berlusconi government, which had in the meantime come into power in 2001, that the articles in the bill designed to make HEIs the sole providers of *formazione* (be it pre-service or in-service) would greatly undermine the capacity of schools to be the places of CPD they were meant to be (CNPI, letter to the Minister of Education, 9 December 2002). The CNPI highlighted the need to capitalise on what teachers and school heads had painstakingly achieved in the preceding years within their own schools and with other schools. Thanks also to the 'strong tradition of experiences' of the *sperimentazione* ('experimentation' or pilot project) phases of the previous three decades, schools in the meantime had been engaging in 'pedagogical reflection [that] had stressed the role of the teacher as researcher and a model of teaching as research' (Dutto, 2000, p. 43). In a number of cases schools were taking a lead in becoming professional development providers for others. Ultimately, the CNPI experts expressed reservations about the marginal roles that 'good teaching practice' would play in professional development if the HEIs were to take over. (Whether or not Italian HEIs are in the best position to serve schools in their improvement efforts is yet another issue that would need careful consideration.) The advice went unheeded. Moreover, nowhere does the 2003 law contemplate CPD or CPL. Once more, the issue of 'Whose agency?' is at stake. *Formazione* seems again to be something 'done to' those most involved.

It appears safe, then, to conclude that, in relation to the universe of professional development in the Italian school system, it is extremely difficult to 'refer to definitions describing things in unequivocal terms, although growing attention is dedicated to research in the sector and to its results' (Spinosi, 2004, p. 348). The difficulty in reaching a consistent use of the terms is simply a sign of the tensions at play and of the co-existence of diverse conceptual paradigms.

### 'Small Incremental Changes' and 'Large Quantum Effects'

The previous two sections have highlighted only some of the challenges facing the CPD scene in/for Italian schools. Other fields of tension, also shared by school improvement efforts in general, are present. Bottom-up initiatives or top-down requirements? Support or pressure? Development or accountability? Right or duty? *Wollen* or *sollen*? (the needs of the individual vs. the requirements of the organisation). All-out networks or all-in packages? Learning cultures or teaching ones? *Apprendimento* or *aggiornamento*? *Flow* or fear? Educational leadership or school management? The policy we want or the politics we get (see Csikszentmihalyi, 1990; MacBeath et al, 2000; Schein, 2003; Schratz, 2004)? As the forces at play loop into each other, 'small incremental changes can produce large quantum effects' (Morgan, 1998, p. 232). Illustrated below are three of the apparently small initial changes now engaging 'critical mass' numbers of people in the Italian school landscape, which have impacted on the way professional development is currently being seen and undertaken in this country.

*Change no. 1: professional development is a right, not an obligation.* In the last 10 years, national teacher contracts and relevant legislation have confronted the professional development issue with three different approaches:

- *aggiornamento* and *formazione* as a 'right' and 'duty' (Testo Unico 297, 1994);
- as an 'obligation' (CCNL, 1995-99);
- as a 'right' for teachers but an 'obligation' for schools in guaranteeing the exercise of this right (CCNL, 1999-2002 and 2002-05), emphasising the professional *responsibility* of both teachers and school leaders in professional development.

The 'carrot and stick' method applied in the second phase ('obligation' by contract in order for teachers to rise on the pay scale) led roughly 90% of the teaching population by 2000 to become involved in forms of professional development, some of it in preparation for the dawn of school autonomy that year (Neri, 2004). This represents a steep increase from 1990, when only 43% of secondary schoolteachers, for instance, were involved in some sort of *aggiornamento* (Grassi, 1999). The third approach of professional development as 'right' would seem to view the school as a mature environment with equally mature professionals who can take charge of their own development. However, it is early to say whether we might truly speak of a new permeating professional development culture. Doubts were expressed earlier in this sense, in relation both to the awareness of the players involved and to the limited range of 'qualified' support providers that schools may be able to turn to in the future (HEIs). What we *can* say is that teachers and heads are finally being treated as professionals who bear the joint responsibility of what they make themselves to be, and their schools to be with them.

*Change no. 2: flexible, accessible, self-directed professional learning turns people on (to learning).* In recent years, more and more experiential learning options have been made available in professional development initiatives for all school staff (teachers, heads, administrative personnel and caretakers). The following comparison illustrates a paradigmatic shift in the ways planning newer forms of professional development have been approached (Figure 1).

Nowhere has this paradigmatic shift become more evident than in the outstanding e-learning feat accomplished in the last five years by the INDIRE (www.indire.it). From the tens of thousands of teachers, tutors and experts engaging in the early online activity of the late 1990s, it has moved into the realms of what the institute's director, Giovanni Biondi, terms 'x-learning', annually involving hundreds of thousands of practitioners, support staff and external experts in sets of networked learning. The approach uses forums, tasks, areas of knowledge management, learning objects, simulations, courseware and individual and group study materials all produced with specific systems of content management for virtual communities (Bartoletti, 2004), in which each atom variably compounds with others to form something 'new' every time. Rather than focusing on content itself, however, 'x-learning' is centred on the learner and presents 'scenarios of integrated learning beyond e-learning ... Everyone learns different things, in a social environment in which the skills acquired are certified ... the knowledge built is acknowledged, and endless learning opportunities are offered' (Biondi, 2003). Participation in online professional dialogue amongst the target groups has been beyond the rosiest expectations (Bartoletti, 2004), showing that Italian teachers and school heads are taking over more and more of their professional development processes and are developing greater ownership of the results, thus building *agency*. The INDIRE portal's webzine and special 'focus' sections also represent a storehouse of information and professional discussion on current education issues, thus feeding into the CPD and CPL of its users.

| from | to |
|------|-----|
| Linear lecture-style training | Interactive, experiential knowledge-building |
| Sequential content matter | Network, modular structure |
| Individualistic/competitive training | Cooperative learning |

Figure 1. The shift from 'training' to 'knowledge building' in PD (after Imperato, 2004).

But this has not been all. The 2003 Education Reform Act has mandated maintenance of portfolios for all children in basic education (ages 6-14). Professional development portfolios have recently been part of the documentary requirements for headship recruitment examinations (in Tuscany, for example). The importance of adult learning experience narratives (Demetrio, 2001) intersects with teachers' desires to 'capture' and narrate their daily professional lives (Barzanò & Pendezzini, 2003). It is no wonder, then, that the Emilia-Romagna Education Authority should come to publish (AIMC et al, 2004) the findings of a teacher-portfolio research project, encased in a CPL perspective, which was carried out in conjunction with the regional branches of the major teacher associations in the country:

> Parallel to the student's portfolio, the teacher's portfolio allows him/her to record and illustrate the most significant events of his/her professional biography, including certified study and diplomas, in-services, participation in research, responsibility-taking positions within schools. However, it focuses particularly on the ways the teacher leads the teaching/learning processes in daily practice, the attention

here being concentrated on the quality of his/her teaching and on the achievements of his/her pupils. (Stellacci, 2004, p. 45)

*Change no. 3: geese fly faster and go further in a flock (MacBeath, 2003).* A quick Google web search at 11 a.m. on 27 July 2004 for *scuole in rete* ('school network', but also 'schools with Internet access') gave 17,100 hits and *rete di scuole* ('a school network') produced 6,600. The same search five minutes later for the English equivalent (school network) struck 14,400. Far from being proof of a comparatively greater interest in school networking in Italy than in the immense English-speaking world, it may be a simple indicator of just how much web talk and documentary evidence there is of it being a *big* issue in the country. One of the fundamental pieces of legislation making Italian schools 'autonomous' (DPR 275, 1999) in 2000 dedicates a 10-comma article (article 7) to *reti di scuole* and to all the different types of collaboration and synergy schools are allowed (and invited) to create with each other and with other players in the community and the wider environment. Amongst these are: 'teaching activities, research, experimentation, development and *formazione* and *aggiornamento*'. There are literally thousands of school networks (MIUR, 2003) now operating in the country, on more or less formal bases, some as clusters of two- or three-school micro-networks (as in the 1999-2002 VIVES project on staff appraisal and curriculum development (www.invalsi.it/vives2/ index0102.htm)) and others even as macro-networks of 100 or more *istituti scolastici* (meaning a school or a cluster of school) (as in the AIR [Autoanalisi d'Istituto in Rete] school self-analysis project, with members in almost every Italian region [www.progettoair.it]). Many of the networks grow mutual and collective learning environments as some of the best examples of CPD in Italy in these years. Some particularly enlightened networks have been able to tap important European Social Fund Objective 3 resources in order to interpret strategic regional development priorities geared to the improvement of the quality of services. One such project, Nuovi Apprendimenti per l'Organizzazione che Apprende (NAPOA) (New Learning for the Learning Organisation), involved 48 schools, three public authorities and four business associations and organisations in three provinces in Lombardy (northern Italy) in a seven-tier initiative that also saw, among other things, the creation of a teachers' resource centre to serve the area and a shared reflective study of the crucial competencies of the 'expert teacher' (Barzanò et al, 2002-03; www.napoa.it).

### Conclusion: eight points to (re)consider

In 1999, the Coordinamento per la Formazione degli Insegnanti (CFI) drew up a list of 10 points that would help schools and the school system 'sharpen their saw' (Covey, 1989), the 'saw' being the human resources that can drive the needed changes (CFI, 1999, cited in Dutto, 2000). The 10 points sketch a new vision of professional development as CPD/CPL then circulating in a number of both grass-roots and policy circles. Two of the points were linked to specific contingencies of the moment, but it is high time to consider the rest anew for the impact they still may have, in Italy and elsewhere. These eight considerations may be rephrased in English as follows, thus comprising a sort of concluding 'manifesto' to this 'Italian response':

- is closely tied to the quality of learning experiences for pupils;
- owning a professional 'biography' allows teachers to keep track of the 'professional discretionary power' they exercise;
- being able to learn and inclined to engage in continuous learning cycles is a fundamental condition for a career-long system of professional learning (*formazione*);
- reflecting *on* practice is one of the non-eliminable dimensions in every development initiative (*formazione*) for learning-centred professions;
- the space teachers have for research is closely tied to the freedom schools have to engage in research;
- the well-being of teachers has rarely appeared as a policy agenda priority;
- the quality of professional development for teachers is closely tied to the quality of learning experiences for pupils;
- the meaning of professional collaboration/collegiality to a great extent requires revisitation;
- professional development (*formazione*) is not a commodity good, but an investment in people (CFI, 1999, cited in Dutto, 2000).

### References

Associazione Italiana Maestri Cattolici (AIMC) et al (Eds) (2004) *Il Portfolio degli Insegnanti: per documentare il curriculum professionale dei docenti.* Bologna: USR Emilia Romagna and IRRE Emilia Romagna.

Bartoletti, l. (2004) PuntoEdu, Quando il Modello è di Successo, *INDIRE Webzine*, 11 May. Available at: www.indire.it

Barzanò, G., Banterle, A., Bettoni, C. et al (Eds) (2002-03) *Percorsi di Sviluppo Professionale per il Personale della Scuola*, 7 vols. Milano: Progetto NAPOA.

Barzanò, G. & Pendezzini, A. (Eds) (2003) *Il Tempo della Ricreazione: racconti di esperienze nell'imparare e nell'insegnare.* Bergamo: QUITE-Grafital.

Biondi, G. (2003) *X-learning? Dall'intervento del Direttore al Salone dell'Educazione a Milano.* Available at: www.indire.it

Brotto, F. (2003) A Three (Four)-year Experiment at Teacher Leadership in Italy. Paper presented at the International Congress of School Effectiveness and Improvement, Sydney, 7 January.

Brotto, F. (2004) Il Tempo Professionale degli Insegnanti. Unpublished paper.

Cerini, G. (2000) A che Punto Siamo con la Formazione degli Insegnanti? Available at: www.edscuola.it/archivio/riformeonline/forma_00.html

Coordinamento per la Formazione degli Insegnanti (CFI) (1999) *Sviluppiamo la Formazione degli Insegnanti.* Rome: Ministero della Pubblica Istruzione.

Covey, S. (1989) *The Seven Habits of Highly Effective People.* London: Simon & Schuster.

Csikszentmihalyi, M. (1990) *Flow: the psychology of optimal experience.* New York: Harper & Row.

Demetrio, D. (2001) L'Apprendimento degli Insegnanti. Talk given to *funzione-obiettivo* teachers, Perugia, 16 May.

Dutto, M.G. (2000) La Formazione Continua degli Insegnanti: ieri, oggi e domani, *Annali della Pubblica Istruzione*, 1-2, pp. 31-49.

Frost, D., Durrant, J., Head, M. & Holden, G. (2000) *Teacher-led School Improvement.* London: RoutledgeFalmer.

Gattullo, M. (1990) Il Profilo Professionale dell'Insegnante, in M. Corda Costa & S. Meghnagi (Eds) *Insegnanti: formazione iniziale e formazione continua*, pp. 330-352. Rome: NIS.

Giddens, A. (1984) *The Constitution of Society.* Cambridge: Polity Press.

Grassi, R. (1999) L'Aggiornamento. I dati della seconda ricerca IARD sugli insegnanti in Italia, *Annali della Pubblica Istruzione,* 3-4, pp. 57-68.

Huber, S. & Schratz, M. (2004) South Tyrol, Italy: qualifying for *dirigente* at a government-selected private provider, in S. Huber (Ed.) *Preparing School Leaders for the 21st Century*, pp. 210-217. London: RoutledgeFalmer.

Imperato, E. (2004) Gli Insegnanti in Italia e in Europa: formazione, valutazione, carriera, in *Formazione, Valutazione, Carriera degli Insegnanti in Italia e in Europa: rapporto di ricerca,* pp. 82-154. Rome: MIUR/Ufficio Scolastico Regionale Lazio.

MacBeath, J. (2003) Self-evaluation, Headship and Leadership: issues from the English-speaking world, in F. Brotto (Tr. and Ed.) Autovalutazione d'Istituto e Leadership a più Voci/Self-evaluation and Schools: whose leadership?, Atti del Convegno/Conference Proceedings, Milan, 20 November. Available at: www.indire.it

MacBeath, J., Schratz, M., Meuret, D. & Jakobsen, L. (2000) *Self-evaluation in European Schools: a story of change.* London: RoutledgeFalmer.

Marczely, B. (1999) *Personalizzare lo Sviluppo Professionale degli Insegnanti.* Trento: Erickson.

Ministero dell'Istruzione, dell'Universita' e della Ricerca (MIUR) (2003) All the Numbers of the Italian Education System, *Quaderni degli Annali dell'Istruzione,* 100.

Morgan, G. (1998) *Images of Organization: the executive edition.* San Francisco: Bennett-Koehler/London: Sage.

Neri, S. (2004) La Formazione degli Insegnanti verso la Scuola dell'Autonomia, in *Formazione, Valutazione, Carriera degli Insegnanti in Italia e in Europa:*

*rapporto di ricerca,* pp. 10-81. Rome: MIUR/Ufficio Scolastico Regionale Lazio.

Organisation for Economic Co-operation and Development (OECD) (2002) Education at a Glance. Chapter D: the learning environment and organization of our schools. Available at: www.oecd.org/EN/links_abstract/0,,EN-links_abstract-604-5-no-no-1239-604,00.html

Schein, E. (2003) *Organisationskultur.* Bergisch Gladbach: EHP. Cited in M. Schratz (2004) Leading and Learning: an odd pair? A Plea for Leadership for Learning, trans. F. Brotto. Unpublished paper.

Schratz, M. (2004) Leading and Learning: an odd pair? A Plea for Leadership for Learning. Unpublished paper.

Scurati, C. (2003) L'Autovalutazione, la Dirigenza Scolastica e Aspetti di Leadership: il contesto italiano, in F. Brotto (Tr. and Ed.) Autovalutazione d'Istituto e Leadership a più Voci/Self-evaluation and Schools: whose leadership?, Atti del Convegno/Conference Proceedings, Milan, 20 November. Available at: www.indire.it

Spinosi, M.(2004) Formazione Insegnanti e Dirigenti, in S. Auriemma (Ed.) *Repertorio 2004 Dizionario Normativo della Scuola,* pp. 346-356. Naples: Tecnodid.

Stellacci, L. (2004) Il Portfolio del Docente, *Innovazione Educativa,* 1-2, pp. 45-46.

Stoll, L., Fink, D. & Earl, L. (2003) *It's about Learning (and It's about Time).* London: RoutledgeFalmer.

CHAPTER 6

# A Continuing Professional Development Framework for Scottish Teachers: steps, stages, continuity or connections?

## FIONA CHRISTIE & JIM O'BRIEN

### Introduction

While an integral part of the United Kingdom, Scotland has long retained its own distinctive approach to education and schooling (Bryce & Humes, 2003). The educational system established by the sixteenth-century religious Reformation has subsequently enjoyed 'a not entirely undeserved reputation for commitment to education' (MacKenzie, 1998, p. 13). During the Thatcher years there were attempts to extend English-derived education policies but, as Humes (2000, p. 103) observes, this generated:

> powerful resistance by the Scottish people to ill-judged
> attempts to assimilate it to English norms. Much of this lies at
> a deep level of national consciousness and is mixed up with
> myth and romanticism. But neither bureaucratic values nor
> institutional structures nor career-minded officials ... have
> been able to extinguish Scotland's desire to retain the
> distinctiveness of its educational system, as an important
> symbol of nationhood.

The reputation of the Scottish education system has endured into modern times but is increasingly being queried and there are demands that Scottish education be awakened:

> from its self-satisfied sleep of reason to face the vast swathes of
> young people, trapped in the forgotten rustbelt housing
> schemes that continue to scar the nation's major conurbations,

> to invite them in to the practical regeneration of their school
> communities. (Davis, 2003, p. 582)

The re-establishment of the Scottish Parliament in 1999, as part of the developing devolved structure of governance in the United Kingdom, provides an opportunity to reassert the importance of education and to further develop a distinctly Scottish approach within the United Kingdom. There is some evidence of increasing independence, as education is the largest devolved service (Bryce & Humes, 2003) and the Scottish Executive Education Department (SEED) oversees policy development increasingly in a spirit of partnership with interested stakeholders. This reflects the new Parliament's desire to share power – 'between parliament and executive, and between them and the people' (Consultative Steering Group, 1998, p. 3). This is evidenced by the developments in teacher continuing professional development (CPD) since 1998.

Teacher education in Scotland is also distinctive (O'Brien, 1996). Historically, for most teachers the experience of 'formal' professional development, beyond courses involving familiarisation and preparation for the curricular reforms of the 1980s and 1990s, was related to planned education authority or in-school activity. This provision was usually associated with the aims and targets of individual school development plans, informed by self-evaluation approaches. Provision was available nationally for staff development and review and extensive management training. Teacher experience of this traditional form of in-service education and training (INSET) 'might fairly be described as voluntary and spasmodic' (O'Brien & Draper, 2003, p. 70). The vast majority of Scottish teachers did not take additional qualifications despite systems of accrediting experience that emerged with new and professionally oriented but elective and voluntary master's and postgraduate diploma/certificate awards (Landon, 1995). There was a growing policy suggestion that this unplanned model of professional development was insufficient.

### Effective CPD

Alongside dissatisfaction with much professional development has grown both an appreciation of the need for teachers to be committed to lifelong learning and an understanding of the nature of effective CPD. The importance being placed on CPD in recent changes to teachers' professional conditions of service in Scotland stems from an analysis of the challenges they face in today's fast-paced world:

> The rapid changes that have taken place in many subjects;
> changes in the curriculum and teaching methods;
> development in technology, particularly information and

communications technology; and the constantly evolving role
of schools in our society, all mean that a teacher's
competences and knowledge need frequently to be reviewed
and updated. (SEED, 2000, p. 8)

Evidence from a range of professions indicates that effective CPD
requires an appropriate support infrastructure and that expectations
should be clearly laid out by professional organisations (Friedman et al,
1999; Phillips et al, 2002). But for teachers the effectiveness of CPD
hangs on the conditions under which opportunities for development
actually result in changes in classroom practice. Harland & Kinder (1997)
suggest that up to nine outcomes must be present, either pre-existing or
following an in-service event: material and provisionary outcomes;
informational outcomes; new awareness; value congruence; affective and
motivational outcomes; attitudinal outcomes; knowledge and skills;
institutional outcomes; and impact on practice. In the three-tier
hierarchy of outcomes they propose *value congruence*, when a teacher's
personal values about what constitutes good teaching match the message
about best practice being promulgated in the in-service provision, and
*knowledge and skills* are 'first order' (Harland & Kinder, 1997, p. 77)
outcomes. Their research indicated that teachers follow an individual
path through the outcomes, the implication being that one in-service
event will lead to different outcomes for different participants.

CPD activities will not be developmental unless they take on 'real
personal value' (Head & Taylor, 1997, p. 6) for participants, engage with
the purposes of the teacher (Hargreaves, 1992) and are sustained and
followed up (Eraut, 1994). Real teacher development needs to be based
on serious teacher talk grounded in a professional community and is
often informal and day-to-day (Feiman-Nemser, 2001). The need for an
appropriate context for development has not been made explicit in the
Scottish CPD framework, which appears to 'focus on teacher
development as an individual enterprise' (Reeves et al, 2002, p. 33).

### The Introduction of Standards and Competences

The first set of competence statements in Scotland, those for initial
teacher education (ITE) courses, were developed following the
expression of a politician's desire to 'reform' initial teacher training, at
least according to one possible version of the 'story' (Stronach et al,
1994). In addition, the profound influence of Her Majesty's Inspectorate
on all aspects of Scottish educational life cannot be underestimated,
particularly before its repositioning outside government as an executive
agency in 2001. Policy on the content, nature and duration of courses
leading to teaching qualifications was published by the Scottish Office
Education Department (1993). These competence-based guidelines were
not uncontroversial but they were relatively quickly implemented by the

Scottish teacher education institutions (Stronach et al, 1994; Christie, 2003a). These guidelines were superseded by benchmark information for ITE, published in 2000 in the wake of the Dearing, Garrick and Sutherland reports into higher and initial teacher education (Christie, 2003a). Such guidelines include the competences expected of the beginning teacher, encompassing knowledge, understanding, critical thinking and practical skills. All ITE courses require the approval of SEED and are professionally accredited by the General Teaching Council for Scotland (GTCS). No blueprint or prescription exists on how such competences are to be covered, nor the order in which they might be introduced. Such decisions are regarded as properly a matter of discussion between the universities, schools and education authorities working in partnership to design and implement relevant programmes which meet the guidelines. An emphasis on partnership and close working relationships between university teacher educators and teachers in schools are deemed critical. There has been criticism of the competence approach (Carr, 1993; Humes, 1995), but the guidelines confirm that the overall aim of courses of ITE is to prepare students to become not only competent but also thoughtful practitioners committed to providing high-quality teaching for all students.

### CPD through Standards

Competences and standards for experienced and expert teachers can be found throughout the developed world, for example Canada, the USA and Australia. Scotland has no equivalent of England's Teacher Training Agency, which has been instrumental in the development of a range of standards for advanced skill teachers, special educational needs (SEN) coordinators and head teachers. The Scottish approach to agreeing statements of competences or standards reflects a professional consensus. Prior to the increasing independence and diversity associated with Scottish education since the re-establishment of the Scottish Parliament, there was a tradition of wide consultation on proposed developments and changes usually through the publication of a paper and a formal associated consultation and evaluation process. Development through such centre-periphery models is regarded suspiciously by some commentators (Purdon, 2003a), who consider such an approach as managed change and pseudo-consultation, but nevertheless Scottish teachers are used to consultative processes that are becoming increasingly inclusive and not reflecting a 'top-down' model. For example, prior to the substantive consultation on the Chartered Teacher initiative, the Scottish Standard for Headship (Scottish Office Education and Industry Department, 1998) initially involved commissioned research (Casteel et al, 1997), followed by a development period including a cycle of consultation. This resulted in the standard being drafted and redrafted in the light of a series of open conferences and discussions with stakeholders including heads and education authority representatives. As a result, important accepted elements in the Scottish Qualification for Headship programme are work-based learning (Reeves et al, 2002) and partnership with education authority and university involvement (Murphy et al, 2002).

In Scotland, as elsewhere, an attempt has been made to create the missing coherence in teachers' professional education and further development using the mechanism of standards. These detail the competences expected at different stages of a teacher's career and provide a framework for associated programmes of CPD. Although standards are often associated with rhetoric about greater teacher professionalism, misgivings have been expressed about the effect of standards on professional autonomy and their limited range. Storey & Hutchinson (2001) see in a framework of standards both a potential threat to the autonomy of teachers and also an opportunity to reprofessionalise. Tickle (2001), writing about the original English induction standards (revised standards were published in 2003), was concerned that they reflected too narrow a view of teacher expertise and that their use would lead to induction becoming assessment- rather than development-led. For Stephens et al (2004, p. 113) the standards-based approach 'fails to take account of what Duncan (1998) calls the messy kind of wisdom: teacher knowledge that can only be acquired in practice and through personal experimentation'. It is not clear why Scottish policy makers have chosen the path of professional development through standards, although suspicions have been expressed that such a framework allows closer political control over teachers' lives, however teacher-friendly the accompanying rhetoric may be (Purdon, 2003a).

The introduction of standards has led to what Patrick et al (2003) identify as two sets of competing discourses in Scottish education, performativity versus autonomy and managerialism versus pedagogic excellence. They suggest that by conceptualising teaching in simplistic terms as a set of measurable outcomes, the CPD framework risks undermining the autonomy and professionalism which it claims to enhance. However, other commentators have come to different conclusions: 'Scottish developments appear to be based on a continuation of a public service ethic, trust in teachers, and an absence of performativity' (Menter et al, 2004, p. 102).

So who is right? Our own research (Draper et al, 2004) on the new induction phase and associated Standard for Full Registration (SFR) would suggest that there is a significant gap between policy and reality, partly because of the hasty implementation of some aspects of the framework. In the absence of clear guidelines and an accompanying debate, teachers have paid lip-service to the requirements of the SFR, for example, without really engaging with the underlying principles. That is not to say that the structure and assumptions of the framework may not, over time, reduce teachers' freedom to act and plan for themselves, ultimately undermining their professional autonomy.

In England, the equivalent standard documents have been placed very firmly within a discourse of performativity. The press release announcing the launching of new Standards for Qualified Teacher Status call them 'the framework against which all trainee teachers *will be judged*' (Teacher Training Agency, 2002; emphasis added). The standards serve to allow gate-keeping to the next phase rather than to facilitate professional growth (Shelton Mayes, 2001). In Northern Ireland, the same drive to integrate various stages of a teacher's early career has resulted in the issuing of a set of developmental competences (rather than standards) within the context of a three-way partnership between higher education institutions (HEIs), schools and regional education and library boards (Kearns, 2001).

### The Emergence of the Scottish CPD Framework

The framework emerging in Scotland promises to provide a coherent structure for quality professional learning at all levels of a teacher's career. A careless observer of Scottish developments might subscribe to the recent development of standards beyond ITE as being part of a series of changes in Scottish teachers' conditions of service designed to raise the status and enhance the professionalism of teachers following the publication of the McCrone Report (SEED, 2000). However, the four standards that underpin the framework for CPD for Scottish teachers have emerged in a piecemeal fashion. Each standard was developed separately and in response to a different set of external influences (Purdon, 2003a; see also Table I for a chronology). As well as the four standards and the additional framework for CPD for educational leaders, another piece of the CPD jigsaw is the requirement that teachers carry out an additional 35 hours of CPD a year. This compares with the 48 hours of CPD in three years required by the Law Society and the minimum of 35 hours per year of CPD activity the Institute of Personnel and Development requires of its members (Friedman et al, 1999).

Questions can be raised about the nature of the professionalism elaborated in the standard documents and by the post-McCrone agreement (SEED, 2001). A closer look at the genesis of the framework and our research into the implementation of a scheme to improve the quality of one of the stages (Christie et al, 2003) also reveal that there is still a significant gap between the rhetoric of 'continuum' and the reality of disjointed and fragmented experience.

| Date | Publication | Comments |
|------|-------------|----------|
| 1993 | Scottish Office Education Department (1993) *Guidelines for Teacher Training Courses* | Initially highly controversial but quickly accepted in practice (Stronach et al, 1994; Christie, 2003a) |
| 1998 | Scottish Office Education and Industry Department (1998) *The Standard for Headship in Scotland* | Followed consultation with head teachers and serves as basis for the Scottish Qualification for Headship (O'Brien et al, 2003) |
| 1998 | Scottish Office Education Department (1998) *Revised Guidelines for Teacher Training Courses* | Minor changes from 1993 document, including responsibility of all teachers for development of numeracy and literacy of all pupils and information and communications technology (replacing radio and television broadcasts) (Christie, 2003a) |
| 2000 | Quality Assurance Agency for Higher Education (2000) *The Standard for Initial Teacher Education in Scotland: benchmark information* | Made necessary by the recommendations of the Dearing and Sutherland reports. Quality Assurance Agency for Higher Education as ITE was to be treated like other university subjects (Christie, 2003a) |
| 2002 | SEED (2002a) *The Standard for Chartered Teacher* | Initially to be Standard for Expert Teacher, became for Chartered Teacher in McCrone and based on very widespread consultation (Christie, 2003a) |
| 2002 | SEED (2002b) *The Standard for Full Registration* | Basis for the induction year and based on sketchy consultation (Purdon, 2003a) |
| 2003 | SEED (2003) *Continuing Professional Development for Educational Leaders* | A suggested framework for CPD for leadership development (O'Brien, 2004) |

Table I. Chronology of events in construction of the Scottish CPD framework.

### Teachers' Fragmented Learning

The recent drive to shape teachers' pre- and in-service learning into a continuum stems from the realisation that for many the reality of professional development has been fragmentary and unsatisfactory throughout (Sutherland, 1997; Humes, 2001; Patrick et al, 2003). Pre-service, student teachers often struggle to integrate the school placement and university-based components of their undergraduate degrees or postgraduate courses (Aitken & Mildon, 1992; Eraut, 1994) and, as beginning teachers, they struggle to link their early experiences of teaching to their pre-service courses (Christie et al, 2003). Some are two or three years into their careers before they can see the point of aspects of their ITE (Humes, 2001). Induction, which ideally would help beginning teachers make connections between theory and practice, has, until recently, often been cursory, concerned merely to socialise teachers into the life of the school (Draper et al, 1991; Feiman-Nemser, 2001).

As they proceed through their careers, teachers may experience in-service provision as 'a set of disconnected and decontextualized experiences' (Feiman-Nemser, 2001, p. 1041), which operate on an ineffective 'deficit-training-mastery model' (Clarke & Hollingsworth, 2002, p. 948). In short, what Feiman-Nemser (2001, p. 1049) calls the 'connective tissue' linking the different phases of a teacher's career has been missing from the experience of many and there have been deficiencies in the professional development available to teachers at every stage.

## McCrone, Standards and Professionalism

In Scotland, the development of standards seemed to have a momentum of its own; although the McCrone Report was to be extremely influential in many other areas, it merely welcomed the work that had already begun in CPD and only indirectly influenced the direction the work took. The chief concern of the McCrone Report seemed to lie with the *quality* of CPD available to teachers, which, apart from the requirement to develop a register of CPD providers, is not apparent in the agreement. The registration of CPD providers has been taken on by the GTCS with the main focus being on the registration of modules for the Chartered Teacher and Scottish Qualification for Headship. The same set of criteria applies to general non-award-bearing short-course CPD provision, not all of which must be registered (GTCS, n.d.)

It is perhaps significant that there is a shift in focus from the McCrone Report to the agreement that followed it. The report merely suggested that teachers would be prepared to commit more of their time to CPD if they could see the benefit to their career. This appears in the agreement as 'a condition of service', as 'a right and responsibility' (can something be both a right and a responsibility?) and as 'professional commitment'. What began life as a proposal that teachers would welcome increased access to high-quality CPD has become a contractual obligation. This might provide support to those who harbour suspicions that the main impetus for the CPD framework was a desire to strengthen political interference in teachers' work.

### Probation to Induction

Research carried out in the 1990s into probation, the two-year 'trial' period at the beginning of Scottish teachers' careers, had raised concerns about the quality of the support being provided and the inadequate development experienced (Draper et al, 1997; McNally, 2002). The Teacher Induction Project, a collaboration between SEED and the GTCS, was established to reform the arrangements for probation and to draft a standard for the completion of probation. Originally intended to dovetail with the 1998 ITE guidelines, the publication of the benchmark information in 2000 provided the framework within which the SFR, published in 2002, was finally developed (Purdon, 2003a).

In addition to the two standard documents, a career entry profile has been developed with a view to enhancing continuity of experience for beginning teachers. This profile is designed to allow HEI staff, along with the student, to record strengths and weaknesses so targets can be set early in the induction year (GTCS, 2002). Our data (Christie et al, 2003) show the profile to have been virtually ignored during the first year of the induction scheme for a variety of reasons.

### Expert Teacher to Chartered Teacher

The development of a Standard for Expert Teacher goes back to the consultation on the development of a national framework of CPD for teachers in Scotland held in 1998. The tender to develop this standard was awarded to a consortium of Arthur Andersen and the universities of Edinburgh and Strathclyde (Kirk et al, 2003). The McCrone Committee, set up in 1999 with a view to finding a way out of an impasse which had developed in pay negotiations and reporting in 2000, proposed the grades of Chartered Teacher and Advanced Chartered Teacher (SEED, 2000). The grade of Chartered Teacher was established in the national agreement that followed the McCrone Report and the Standard for Chartered Teacher was published in 2002 (SEED, 2001; Christie, 2003b).

The process of consultation which resulted in the publication of the SFR and Standard for Chartered Teacher has come under scrutiny. There is general agreement that consultation on the Chartered Teacher was wide-ranging and thorough (Christie, 2003a; Kirk et al, 2003), although perhaps only because it was going to have to prove its value in the marketplace (Purdon, 2003a). Consultation on the SFR was much less transparent, with few changes being made to the draft following the consultation and the final version delivered to schools as a *fait accompli* (Purdon, 2003b). More fundamentally, there has been no consultation on the *concept* of a standards-based reform of CPD. For some observers this indicates a tacit acceptance by the profession that ultimate political control of CPD rests with SEED (Purdon, 2003a).

### Headship and Educational Leadership

The Standard for Headship dates from 1998 and was developed to fulfil a commitment made in the 1997 Labour manifesto to develop qualifications and training for the post of head teacher (Kirk et al, 2003). The process of development of the Standard for Headship followed a characteristically Scottish model of 'managed consultation' with a development group producing a draft to which groups of head teachers then responded (O'Brien et al, 2003).

As well as seeking to provide coherence in the development of teachers, a national committee was established to offer guidance on how leadership and management skills should be further developed. This committee has now reported after consultation with the teaching profession and the report begins by helpfully defining the relationship between leader and manager:

> A leader secures the support, commitment and enthusiasm of staff and so enables the smooth and effective running of often-complex systems of management. Leadership is about defining what the future should look like, agreeing a shared vision and inspiring others to make it happen, even in the face of adversity ... Management, however, might more appropriately be viewed as the practical application of leadership skills. Effective leadership provides positive direction and purpose. Effective management ensures that purpose can be achieved. (SEED, 2003, p. 4)

In addition, a framework for development has been agreed that identifies four broad levels through which progression in educational leadership takes place:

- project leadership (time-limited, small-scale projects for teachers early in their career);
- team leadership (permanent teams of staff or regular leadership of working groups);
- school leadership (including the soon to be mandatory Scottish Qualification for Headship);
- strategic leadership (for those with overall responsibility for a school, or engaged in leading major initiatives at a local or national level).

Does this framework inspire confidence? Will it ensure the kind of development opportunities needed if Scottish schools are to be well led and managed in a changing world? For the first time a model of progression is provided but, while welcome, it has limitations. By setting out exemplars of actions and development activities illustrating 'the competences characteristic of effective leadership' (O'Brien, 2004, p. 2), it succeeds in blurring distinctions between management and leadership.

It also establishes for many a direct relationship between the four levels of leadership and four levels of management post within Scottish schools, namely:

- project: main grade teacher (seeking further experience/ responsibility);
- team: principal teacher;
- school: deputy head teacher;
- strategic: head teacher.

This suggests that leadership is for some teachers only because of allied functions and management responsibilities. Individual leadership development needs are likely to be, at least in part, conditioned by issues of career and current responsibility. Acting head teachers, longstanding deputes who do not wish to be heads, aspiring young teachers who wish to develop as fast as they can, experienced head teachers who have reached their first plateau of achievement – these and other groups will have quite specific needs related to their current role, as well as the more generalised and recurring issues of practice.

Will appropriate development experiences be available and be sufficient? We have learned that development programmes such as the Scottish Qualification for Headship, with its strong emphasis on developing and improving practice through self-evaluative ownership of the learning, succeed best in a school context where the pre-existing school culture is already in tune with the improvement model espoused. Significant problems can be caused for the learners in work-based learning programmes in which the learner is isolated within a school culture which does not support the improvement proposed (Reeves et al, 2002). O'Brien et al (2003, p. 72) argued that 'Such frameworks can offer a useful template within which to situate desirable career development at different stages, but should not be used to limit and constrain development'.

This particular framework on leadership, just as with the standards underpinning the CPD framework, may prove to be more of a strait-jacket and more limiting than its designers probably intended it to be.

### Steps or Stages, Continuity or Connections?

It is ironic that a set of initiatives designed to promote greater coherence and professionalism has itself been constructed in such a piecemeal fashion and in a way that may actually undermine the professionalism of teachers. The accepted terminology associated with the overall development is 'framework'. This might suggest ideas such as a scaffold or ladders of opportunities with steps or stages. These might usefully provide continuity or connect together to facilitate teacher lifelong learning and professional development. Now that the framework is in place, will it in fact facilitate greater coherence or has the entire development been a series of disconnected items that have now conveniently and conceptually been bundled together in the haste to provide a series of standards designed to control rather than empower the Scottish teaching profession?

Let us consider the transition from ITE to the induction scheme and subsequent CPD. The framers of the SFR have related the statements in the SFR to the Standard for Initial Teacher Education by showing where new teachers must consolidate or extend their competence or where the competence is new. In some cases newly qualified teachers have both to consolidate and to extend the competence. These are relatively imprecise terms and it is difficult to imagine what the difference in practice would be between them. More critically, for the standards to facilitate a progression from ITE to the first year in teaching, those who assess against the SFR and/or use it to construct programmes of CPD must have a good working knowledge of the ITE standard. Our research indicates that there is widespread ignorance in schools where the SFR is being implemented about the content of ITE programmes, let alone the detail of the benchmark statements. Merely producing documentation in which connections are made is not in itself to guarantee that beginning teachers experience their progress as being along a continuum.

It is also unclear how subsequent professional development, in particular the 35-hour requirement, is meant to be supported within the general CPD framework once a teacher early in their career has completed the SFR and before more experienced teachers embark on the Chartered Teacher programme (usually after five years of experience). The chief executive of the GTCS has hinted that the SFR should play a role beyond initial entry to the profession:

> It [the SFR] sets out clearly what is expected of new teachers during their induction process and it provides a professional standard against which decisions will be taken on full registration. *But the standard will do more than that.* It is also an important element in constructing a national framework for continuing professional development for all teachers. There is, therefore, now a real opportunity here in Scotland to create a continuum of professional development, starting with initial teacher education, being further developed in the new one year induction period and then continuing throughout the rest of a teacher's professional career. (MacIver, 2003, p. 1019; emphasis added)

However, it is unclear what this might mean in practice. What seems to be implied is that the standard will continue to be used in some way beyond the first year of a teacher's career, perhaps to structure an individual's CPD. Our research shows that many teachers working with probationers on the induction scheme were still to be convinced about the worth of the SFR in evaluating and supporting new teachers. New teachers, too, did not tend to engage with the SFR to any depth, which makes it unlikely that these teachers, at least, will turn to the SFR to structure their CPD later in their careers.

Teachers are more likely to experience coherence in their professional development by making *connections* themselves between the different phases and contexts of their careers than by following an externally imposed set of standards. Rather than working their way up a series of *steps*, as marked out by the standards, teachers look for different kinds of development at different *stages* in their careers. Some stages will be marked by more formal learning against criteria laid out in the appropriate standard while others will be characterised by informal learning from colleagues of a kind that is hard to match against a competence statement. The national agreement highlights the central role of teachers in the quality and effectiveness of learning and the Standard for Chartered Teacher (SEED, 2002a, p. 1) itself states that:

> The quality of the educational service depends pre-eminently
> on the quality of our teachers. If higher standards are to be
> achieved and all pupils are to be effectively supported in
> achieving their best potential, it is essential that teachers are
> well prepared for their work and that they have opportunities
> to extend and revitalise their skills throughout their career.

Government is interested and has promoted CPD, including the concept of critical reflection, not just instrumental skill development, because of the overpowering desire to improve schools; it is anticipated that teachers who engage in CPD become more critically reflective at all the stages of the framework. When considering what constitutes professionalism for teachers, Humes (2001, p. 15) asks the question: 'What is it that teachers profess?' and goes on to suggest:

> It is doubtful if most teachers would answer that question by
> saying that they profess a set of competences or a list of
> benchmarks. A more likely response is that they would appeal
> to values and principles concerned with such things as the
> worthwhileness of learning, their commitment to helping
> youngsters develop, their desire to help them achieve, their
> belief in education as a fundamental right, its importance for
> democracy and social justice (see Sutherland 2000). Provision
> for CPD should allow teachers to explore these fundamental
> aims and values.

Certainly each of the standards has a concern about values and professionalism. Equally there is a commitment to extend more democratic processes to school management and leadership (O'Brien et al, 2003); but however much policy makers attempt to portray the current CPD framework as providing a coherent scaffold around which Scottish teachers can structure their professional development, it is possible that, at best, it will serve as a menu. Post-registration, teachers will select the stage of the framework that currently suits their circumstances and ambitions. At other times, the realities of school life and a teacher's individual interests and needs rather than demands of the standards will determine the CPD opportunities teachers select.

For the framework to have a profound effect on the way teachers conceive of CPD, it would have had to have been the result of a more genuinely consultative process as a framework. Thereafter, a much more concerted effort would have been required to allow teachers and education authority staff, in partnership with staff from HEIs, to engage with the standards and the issues they raise. As for a continuum of professional learning, the reality of teachers' careers and learning makes such an apparently desirable goal unattainable. Instead, encouraging teachers as individuals and communities to set their own agendas of professional development within or outwith an external framework allows them to make the connections they need for their own practice while bolstering their professional autonomy.

### References

Aitken, J. & Mildon, D. (1992) Teacher Education and the Developing Teacher: the role of personal knowledge, in M. Fullan & A. Hargreaves (Eds) *Teacher Development and Educational Change*, pp. 10-35. London: Falmer Press.

Bryce, T. & Humes, W. (2003) *Scottish Education: second edition, post devolution.* Edinburgh: Edinburgh University Press.

Carr, D. (1993) Guidelines for Teacher Training: the competency model, *Scottish Educational Review*, 25(1), pp. 17-25.

Casteel, V., Forde, C., Reeves, J. & Lynas, R. (1997) *A Framework for Leadership and Management Development in Scottish Schools.* Glasgow: Quality in Education, University of Strathclyde.

Christie, D. (2003a) Competences, Benchmarks and Standards in Teaching, in T. Bryce & W. Humes (Eds) *Scottish Education: second edition, post devolution*, pp. 952-963. Edinburgh: Edinburgh University Press.

Christie, D. (2003b) Assessing Teachers' Professional Development Using the New Standard for Chartered Teacher in Scotland. Paper given at the British Educational Research Association Annual Conference, Edinburgh, 11-13 September.

Christie, F., Draper, J. & O'Brien, J. (2003) *A Study of the Induction Scheme for Beginning Secondary Teachers in Scotland.* Edinburgh: Centre for Educational Leadership, University of Edinburgh.

Clarke, D. & Hollingsworth, H. (2002) Elaborating a Model of Teacher Professional Growth, *Teaching and Teacher Education,* 18(8), pp. 947-967.

Consultative Steering Group (1998) *Shaping Scotland's Parliament.* Edinburgh: Scottish Office.

Davis, R.A. (2003) Education, Utopia and the Limits of Enlightenment, *Policy Futures in Education,* 1(3), pp. 565-585.

Draper, J., Fraser, H., Smith, D. & Taylor, W. (1991) *A Study of Probationers.* Edinburgh: Moray House Institute.

Draper, J., Fraser, H., Raab, A. & Taylor, W. (1997) *Probationers on Supply.* Edinburgh: Edinburgh University/GTCS.

Draper, J., O'Brien, J. & Christie, F. (2004) First Impressions: the new teacher induction arrangements in Scotland, *Journal of In-service Education,* 30(2), pp. 201-223.

Duncan, B. (1998) On Teacher Knowledge: a return to Shulman, in *Philosophy of Education Yearbook 1998*, electronic source 1-3. Urbana-Champaign: University of Illinois, Philosophy of Education Society.

Eraut, M. (1994) *Developing Professional Knowledge and Competence.* London: Falmer Press.

Feiman-Nemser, S. (2001) From Preparation to Practice: designing a continuum to strengthen and sustain teaching, *Teachers' College Record,* 103(6), pp. 1013-1055.

Friedman, A., Hurran, N. & Durkin, C. (1999) Good Practice in CPD among UK Professional Associations, *Continuing Professional Development,* 2, pp. 52-68.

General Teaching Council for Scotland (GTCS) (n.d.) General Criteria for CPD. Available at: http://www.gtcs.org.uk/cpd.aspx?MenuItemID=114&ID =&selection=4

General Teaching Council for Scotland (GTCS) (2002) *Achieving the Standard for Full Registration: guidance for schools.* Edinburgh: GTCS.

Hargreaves, A. (1992) Cultures of Teaching: a focus for change, in A. Hargreaves & M. Fullan (Eds) *Understanding Teacher Development*, pp. 216-240. London: Cassell.

Harland, J. & Kinder, K. (1997) Teachers' Continuing Professional Development: framing a model of outcomes, *Journal of In-service Education,* 23(1), pp. 71-84.

Head, K. & Taylor, P. (1997) *Readings in Teacher Development.* Oxford: Heinemann.

Humes, W.M. (1995) From Disciplines to Competencies: the changing face of professional studies in teacher education, *Education in the North,* New Series 3, pp. 39-47.

Humes, W. (2000) State: the governance of Scottish education 1872-2000, in H. Holmes (Ed.) *Education.* Vol. 11 of *Scottish Life and Society*. East Lothian: Tuckwell Press in association with European Ethnological Research Centre.

Humes, W. (2001) Conditions for Professional Development, *Scottish Educational Review*, 33(1), pp. 6-17.

Kearns, H. (2001) Competence-based Early Professional Development: first impressions of the Northern Ireland programme, *Journal of In-service Education*, 27(1), pp. 65-82.

Kirk, G., Beveridge, W. & Smith, I. (2003) *The Chartered Teacher*. Edinburgh: Dunedin Academic Press.

Landon, J. (1995) In-service and Professional Development: the emergence of post-graduate award schemes, in J. O'Brien (Ed.) *Current Changes and Challenges in European Teacher Education: Scotland,* pp. 55-65. Brussels: Moray House Institute of Education Professional Development Centre in association with COMPARE-TE European Network.

MacIver, M. (2003) The General Teaching Council for Scotland, in T. Bryce & W. Humes (Eds) *Scottish Education: second edition, post devolution*, pp. 1016-1021. Edinburgh: Edinburgh University Press.

MacKenzie, M.L. (1998) Education and the Governance of Scotland, *Education in the North*, New Series 6, pp. 13-19.

McNally, J. (2002) Developments in Teacher Induction in Scotland and Implications for the Role of Higher Education, *Journal of Education for Teaching*, 28(2), pp. 149-164.

Menter, I., Mahony, P. & Hextall, I. (2004) Ne'er the Twain Shall Meet? Modernizing the Teaching Profession in Scotland and England, *Journal of Education Policy,* 19(2), pp. 195-214.

Murphy, D., Draper, J., O'Brien, J. & Cowie, M. (2002) Local Management of the Scottish Qualification for Headship (SQH), *Journal of In-service Education,* 28(2), pp. 277-295.

O'Brien, J. (Ed.) (1996) *Current Changes and Challenges in European Teacher Education: Scotland.* Brussels: Moray House Institute of Education Professional Development Centre in association with COMPARE-TE European Network.

O'Brien, J. (2004) Leadership Development, *Leading Matters* (Centre for Educational Leadership and Management, Griffith University, Brisbane), 3(1), pp. 1-2.

O'Brien, J. & Draper, J. (2003) Frameworks for CPD: the chartered teacher initiative in Scotland, *Professional Development Today,* 6(Winter), pp. 69-75.

O'Brien, J., Murphy, D. & Draper, J. (2003) *School Leadership*. Edinburgh: Dunedin Academic Press.

Patrick, F., Forde, C. & McPhee, A. (2003) Challenging the 'New Professionalism': from managerialism to pedagogy? *Journal of In-service Education,* 29(2), pp. 237-254.

Phillips, M., Cruickshank, I. & Friedman, A. (2002) *Continuing Professional Development: evaluation of good practice.* Bristol: Professional Associations Research Network.

Purdon, A. (2003a) A National Framework of CPD: continuing professional development or continuing policy dominance?, *Journal of Education Policy,* 18(4), pp. 423-437.

Purdon, A. (2003b) The Professional Development of Teachers, in T. Bryce & W. Humes (Eds) *Scottish Education: second edition, post devolution*, pp. 942-951. Edinburgh: Edinburgh University Press.

Quality Assurance Agency for Higher Education (2000) *The Standard for Initial Teacher Education in Scotland: benchmark information*. Gloucester: Quality Assurance Agency for Higher Education.

Reeves, J., Forde, C., O'Brien, J., Smith, P. & Tomlinson, H. (2002*) Performance Management in Education: improving practice*. London: Paul Chapman Publishing in association with British Educational Leadership and Management Society (BELMAS).

Scottish Executive Education Department (SEED) (2000) *A Teaching Profession for the 21st Century (the McCrone Report)*. Edinburgh: SEED.

SEED (2001) *A Teaching Profession for the 21st Century: agreement reached following recommendations made in the McCrone Report*. Edinburgh: SEED.

SEED (2002a) *The Standard for Chartered Teacher*. Edinburgh: SEED.

SEED (2002b) *The Standard for Full Registration*. Edinburgh: SEED.

SEED (2003) *Continuing Professional Development for Educational Leaders*. Edinburgh: SEED.

Scottish Office Education and Industry Department (1998) *The Standard for Headship in Scotland*. Stirling: Scottish Qualification for Headship Development Unit.

Scottish Office Education Department (1993) *Guidelines for Teacher Training Courses*. Edinburgh: Scottish Office Education Department.

Scottish Office Education Department (1998) *Revised Guidelines for Teacher Training Courses*. Edinburgh: Scottish Office Education Department.

Shelton Mayes, A. (2001) National Standards for Teachers: twenty-first century possibilities for professional development, in F. Banks & A. Shelton Mayes (Eds) *Early Professional Development for Teachers*, pp. 64-70. London: David Fulton.

Stephens, P., Tonnessen, F. & Kyriacou, C. (2004) Teacher Training and Teacher Education in England and Norway: a comparative study of policy goals, *Comparative Education*, 40(1), pp. 109-130.

Storey, A. & Hutchinson, S. (2001) The Meaning of Teacher Professionalism in a Quality Control Era, in F. Banks & A. Shelton Mayes (Eds) *Early Professional Development for Teachers*, pp. 41-53. London: David Fulton.

Stronach, I., Cope, P., Inglis, B. & McNally, J. (1994) The SOED 'Competence' Guidelines for Initial Teacher Training: issues of control, performance and relevance, *Scottish Educational Review*, 26(2), pp. 118-133.

Sutherland, S. (1997) *Teacher Education and Training. Report 10 of the Dearing Report*. London: HMSO.

Sutherland, S. (2000) *Portrait of a Teacher*. The GTCS annual lecture, unpublished.

Teacher Training Agency (2002) Flexibility is Key to High Quality Teacher Training. Available at: http://www.tta.gov.uk/php/ read.php?sectionid=18&articleid=50

*Fiona Christie & Jim O'Brien*

Tickle, L. (2001) Professional Qualities and Teacher Induction, *Journal of In-service Education,* 27(1), pp. 51-64.

CHAPTER 7

# Learning at Work: possible lessons from Canada and the United Kingdom?

## ALEX ALEXANDROU, JOHN DWYFOR DAVIES & JOHN LEE

### Aim

Union learning representatives (ULRs) are a relatively recent phenomenon and are a new category of lay representation within the workplace in the United Kingdom. They are part of the present New Labour administration's drive to expand and improve lifelong learning and create the new 'learning society', in this case particularly amongst the working population by working in partnership with the trade union movement. This initiative has been given greater credence by the Employment Act 2002, which grants a number of statutory rights to ULRs.

The aim of this chapter is twofold: firstly, to explore the new and unique workplace and lifelong learning initiative in the United Kingdom that is the ULRs in both a public service and large industrial setting; and secondly, to compare its operation with a global company's (McDonald's) training for workplace skills programme in Canada.

### Introduction

The United Kingdom is unique in the developed world in that it has established by law the right for workers to elect ULRs. This was achieved through the Employment Act 2002 and puts ULRs on a statutory footing (as of April 2003). Not only does it give recognised trade unions the right to appoint ULRs, the legislation also allows them to have paid leave to train and perform their duties. Of equal significance, and unusually in the case of the United Kingdom, it has given a right to employees not given in the rest of the European Community, where in many other respects workers have rights denied those in the United Kingdom (Vincenzi & Fairhurst, 2002).

The data on ULRs need to be seen in the context of the trade union movement's historic and continuing commitment to education. As the Trades Union Congress (TUC) Learning Services (2004) points out:

> Since their creation, trade unions have always taken their role
> in the Learning Agenda and the ensuing workforce
> development issues very seriously; campaigning for better
> schooling, for technical education, for leisure-time learning
> and for the education of union officials. After the 1999 Moser
> Report [Moser, 1999], which clearly stated a pressing need for
> the country to up skill – highlighting 7 million adults with
> basic skills difficulties, trade unions added the all-important
> lifelong learning for their members and colleagues to that list.

From central government's point of view, the creation of the Union Learning Fund (ULF) was a response for the need for upskilling announced in *The Learning Age* Green Paper (Department for Education and Employment (DfEE), 1998). As the National Literacy Trust (2003) and the Labour Research Department (LRD) (2001) both note, the ULF was established as part of the DfEE's strategy to encourage a culture of lifelong learning through developing workplace initiatives and to boost the unions' capacity as learning organisations.

McDonald's (the global fast-food empire) is well known for its provision of employee training. It has an organisational commitment to the development of employee learning to meet the skills and knowledge needs of the company. These are expressed as a commitment to 'learning development and personal growth' such that 'employees receive work experience that teaches skills and values that last a lifetime' and 'are provided the tools they need to develop personally and professionally' (McDonald's, 2004). McDonald's commitment, on the surface, is similar to what in the United Kingdom is termed 'lifelong learning' – a principle embodied in the development of ULRs. In both cases, what is being stressed is that workers can and should engage with further education, regardless of their qualifications and experience on entry.

### Government Policy and the Development of ULRs

The Department for Education and Skills (DfES) (2002) notes that the ULF has helped to pave the way for the introduction and development of ULRs and to establish a nation-wide network which currently stands at around 9000 trained learning representatives, a number which is expected to rise to over 22,000 by 2010.

Up to and including the 2003-04 financial year, the fund has been allocated almost £40 million (National Literacy Trust, 2003) and, until April 2003, the fund was administered by the DfES (and its predecessor), after which responsibility was transferred to the Learning and Skills Council.

Further credence and authority were given to both the unions and the ULRs in the Department for Trade and Industry (DTI) and DfEE White Paper entitled *Opportunity for All in a World of Change* (DTI & DfEE, 2001). This dealt with the issues of enterprise, skills and innovation, which it regarded as the vital next steps to securing viable and sustainable economic growth and success for the first decade of the new millennium. It argued that:

> Unions and workforce representatives have a crucial role to play in common cause with employers to ensure that individuals have the portable skills they need whilst meeting the immediate needs of business. We are committed as a Government to ensuring that Union Learning Representatives can play their part in both the competitiveness of the enterprise and the personal investment and gains for the employee for lifelong learning. (DTI & DfEE, 2001, paragraph 2.42)

### ULRs: the next step in workplace employee development and learning

We believe from both a United Kingdom and North American perspective that the introduction and development of ULRs is the next crucial step in pursuing an agenda of lifelong learning within the workplace and is part of the continuing process of employers and trade unions coming together to achieve this. It builds on the good work of the Ford Employee Development Assistance Programme (EDAP) in the United Kingdom and the Institute for Career Development (ICD) in the USA.

The Ford EDAP initiative was set up in 1987 as part of that year's pay and conditions agreement. Its primary aim at the time was to improve the poor industrial relations situation between management and the unions. Relations did improve significantly, but this was as a by-product and the key drivers were the opportunity to return to learning, healthier lifestyles and career development. In a nutshell the programme ensures that all Ford employees are eligible for an annual grant of up to £200 to spend on a course that can be either educational or recreational and that will be undertaken on a voluntary basis, in the employee's own time and is distinct and separate from any job-related training that is provided by the company (Lee, 1998).

The findings of Lee (1998), Maguire & Horrocks (1995) and Mortimer (1990), who have evaluated the EDAP scheme, note positive developments and experiences. The key for most observers is the role of the trade unions. They have embraced EDAP, given it their full support and backing and encouraged their members to take advantage of it. As John Monks, the recently retired general secretary of the TUC, stated, education and learning have been core elements of trade union and TUC business ever since the TUC's inception: 'there has been a continuing belief that improving skills will improve opportunities for union members' (TUC, 2001, p. 3).

As for the ICD, Rose et al (2004, pp. 3-4) explain that it grew:

> out of the economic devastation in the 1980s, when thousands of skilled steelworkers lost their jobs and were unable to apply their specific job skills to other industries. While tough times have recently re-emerged in the steel industry, for the past 11 years, steelworkers have been committing as much as 121,000 hours a year to voluntary instruction at 50 steel mill learning centres. The United Steelworkers of America (USWA) first proposed a joint labor/management education program to 13 domestic companies in 1989. The union deemed basic skills as portable enough to protect workers from future dislocation while employers agreed that workers learning on their own time could lead to improved productivity and employee morale.

We believe that these initiatives bode well for workplace learning and will seek to demonstrate that a positive attitude from both management and unions has beneficial effects for the productivity and performance of organisations and the educational well-being of employees.

### The ULR

For the purposes of this chapter, it is important to understand who ULRs are and what their role is. They are lay representatives of unions who receive no financial remuneration apart from expenses accrued in pursuance of their activities. According to the TUC (2001), anyone can become a learning representative, either by volunteering for the role or by being elected by fellow union members. The representatives do not need to have an academic background and many have become ULRs in order to take advantage of a learning opportunity.

ULRs are trained either by their own union or by the TUC in order to ensure that they can support the learning of their work colleagues. At this point, the TUC (2002, p. 8) reports success in the recruitment and training of ULRs – at a point where their 'role is innovative and continuing to develop'. It outlines the key roles of the learning representatives as follows:

- providing learning advice and guidance to employees;
- assisting employees to access funding, for example Individual Learning Accounts (ILAs) and collective learning funds;
- supporting innovative workplace developments such as ULF projects;
- raising employee awareness of the benefits of learning;
- working with employers to identify learning needs;
- negotiating learning agreements with employers including time off for study;
- securing equal opportunities in learning;
- helping employers to establish learning centres/broking provision with colleges;
- monitoring quality of provision.

As the TUC (2002) highlights, the ULRs do receive wide-ranging support for their activities. They are given initial training for their role through courses provided by the TUC, which are accredited by the Open College Network. Over a third of representatives have received additional training in areas such as supporting colleagues with basic skill needs and the ULRs are receiving increasing levels of support in the form of updates and further training from either the TUC's own Learning Services division or individual union learning representative co-ordinators. This concern for training is also evident in the way that McDonald's has attempted to ensure quality and progression through its own organisational lead learning patterns (McDonald's, 2004).

### Earliest Evaluations

Both the TUC and individual unions have been eager to keep track of and to evaluate the role and function of ULRs. The first substantive evaluation was undertaken by the TUC (Cowen et al, 2000). It sought to ask about the early impact of ULRs – more important for our purposes, it asked what advice they were asked for and what kind of support and training they needed. In the case of advice, the evaluation discovered that ULRs were being treated as the kind of people who could open up lifelong learning, something confirmed in our case study of the Public and Commercial Services Union (PCS). At this early stage, the impact was difficult to gauge but there was an enthusiasm for learning amongst the representatives themselves. As a result of the evaluation, it was argued that a learning agenda for representatives based on the TUC premise that negotiating a learning agreement with an employer is as important as negotiating pay and conditions.

The LRD (2003) argued that the agenda should include some or all of the following:

- a commitment from both parties to lifelong learning;
- the number of learning representatives and how the union will appoint them;
- the amount of paid time off for learning representatives to carry out their duties, and undertake training;
- the type and form of training;
- the amount of time off permitted for access time for union members to engage their ULRs and when it could be paid time off;
- the procedure for requesting time off;
- the procedure for resolving disputes over time off;
- payment for time off and whether payment might be made to shift and part-time employees undertaking trade union duties outside their normal working hours;
- facilities for learning representatives such as a room to conduct interviews, use of a telephone, e-mail, Internet and notice boards, etc.;
- the establishment of a joint learning committee comprising equal numbers of union and employer representatives;
- the undertaking of learning needs surveys;
- regular promotional activities regarding learning;
- regular dissemination of information on training and learning opportunities;
- access to training provision.

In order to examine the impact of the ULRs and how much of the above agenda has been taken on board, we now turn to our three case studies.

### The Case Studies

*Background to the Trade Unions and the Company*

The PCS is one of the United Kingdom's largest trade unions. Its members deliver governmental services in both the public and private sectors. The PCS has 288,000 members. They work in government departments, agencies, public bodies and a number of private companies, notably in information technology (PCS, 2004).

Amicus is the major trade union for all workers in the engineering sector and is the largest manufacturing union in the United Kingdom with well over one million members in both the public and private sectors. Its membership covers workers who range from semi-skilled to high-level technicians (Amicus, 2004).

McDonald's started trading in 1948 and it can safely be said that it is the largest and most well-known global fast-food organisation. It has 26,000 outlets in approximately 120 countries and in 2000 it registered more than 17 billion customer visits. It has its own university appropriately named the Hamburger University based at its headquarters in Oak Brook, IL, with 16 full-time international resident professors, and to date more than 73,000 employees have graduated from the university (McDonald's, 2004).

## Methodology

The PCS has engaged in an early evaluative survey of the role of ULRs (PCS Organising and Learning Services, 2003) and it was our intention to triangulate the interview data with the union's own ULR evaluation study and policy documents and compare them with the information from the other two case studies.

With regard to the PCS, interview data were collected from learning representatives attending a training course at PCS headquarters. They were asked for their permission, which they readily gave, and were interviewed in a group, the first a group of seven and the second a group of eight. In the first group there were six females, of whom two had origins in the Indian subcontinent, and one male. In the second group there were two males and one female of Indian subcontinental origin. As a group in this circumstance they were constituted by the discourse of trade unionism and its educational ideals and aspirations.

In the case of both Amicus and McDonald's we had a sole informant. Our Amicus participant was an interesting case, as the role of the ULR from the perspective of our informant, while encompassing the generic role set out in legislation and policy, had some interesting differences. Our informant was a technician employed in the aerospace industry and, as such, already had high levels of knowledge and skills. The McDonald's participant is currently the national director for training, learning and development in Canada. Our informant started off his career as a member of a restaurant crew and now occupies a national executive position, which we believe is significant in the context of our discussion and which we will elaborate on in the case study.

As researchers we decided to record not individual voices but the voices of those in the role of learning representative and director of training, learning and development. We treat the voices as a collective: 'My voice can mean, but only with others: at times in chorus, but at the best of times in a dialogue' (Bakhtin, 1981, p. 165).

The first group of PCS representatives was interviewed by two of the researchers, the second by one researcher. The Amicus representative was interviewed by one of the researchers in a face-to-face interview and the McDonald's participant was interviewed over the telephone by another of the researchers. In each case field notes and tape recording were used. Tape recordings were subsequently transcribed.

A semi-structured interview/discussion schedule was drawn up using the policy documents on ULRs and the evaluation study produced by the PCS (Prime R&D, 2000; PCS, 2002, 2003a; PCS Organising and Learning Services, 2003). The method chosen aimed to move from interviewing and towards open conversation and discussion; as a consequence the researchers sought to facilitate a dialogic discourse (Bakhtin, 1981). In order to do this, it was important to create a conversational rather than an interview scenario. Fortunately we were able to talk with the PCS informants over a sandwich lunch and outside the semi-formal structure of the training session and were able to have conversations with the Amicus and McDonald's participants in informal and non-threatening environments.

We were interested to find out why these workers and the director had taken on their respective challenging roles, how they viewed them and how employees were benefiting from these workplace learning initiatives. The following is representative of what the participants said.

### The PCS Learning Representatives (Mandarins)

This is a woman who had returned to work after having children:

> I'm just enthusiastic about learning new things. [On the tape can be heard murmurs of agreement.] Just dying to get out and do something with my brain ... well computers are challenging so I looked for myself and enrolled on an OU [Open University] course.

In a similar vein another female respondent said:

> Well I've always been curious but I left school and had a family but I couldn't wait to get back to something and this well it's for but it's helping people.

This desire for personal educational development was a feature of all our responses. Not all of them went as far as registering for Open University courses but they all wanted more than just skills updating related to work. Typically a male respondent commented on learning computer skills:

> Well we need better skills because of computers and IT [information technology] but you can do that and get things for yourself like when you do CLAIT [Computer Literacy and Information Technology] 1 and 2.

An original motivation, then, is a desire for what used to be called self-improvement. There is of course a long history of trade unions seeking to ensure that their members have access to education, not just skills related to the work of trade unions but related to liberal education, as the continued trade union commitment to the Workers' Educational Association and Ruskin College demonstrates. PCS Rules and Constitution Object 1g states as a role of the union '[to] promote the educational and cultural well being of members' (PCS, 2003b, p. 2).

In line with this all of our informants were eager to improve their own education in the broadest sense. This general desire for learning is reflected in what the ULRs said their members asked them about, while their role as set out in statute and in the surrounding guidance documents is to interact with colleagues and encourage them to update their workplace skills:

> I've been asked about all sorts of things you know flower arranging, keep fit and that.

We were interested to know whether the ULRs felt they needed to know about the wide range of course available through adult and community education and further education. To this they answered:

> Yes we do find about other courses ... you can get leaflets and that from colleges and the union has them as well. I think that once people get used to us they'll ask for more so we will need more training.

The PCS survey of its own learning representatives reveals a rather similar picture. The survey received 94 replies out of 209, just under 30%. The wish list reported by the ULRs contained art and craft, maths, tap dancing and aromatherapy among the 12 items specified (PCS Organising and Learning Services, 2003). This focus on 'liberal education' is important in maintaining the enthusiasm and motivation of both ULRs and their members and we will return to this later.

### Amicus (Jet Fighters)

Our informant was at pains to explain that he worked in a large and complex industrial plant and that the way in which ULRs were organised was analogous to the way the union organised its general representation. His role was described as 'senior learning rep', and so he had some responsibility to organise and co-ordinate ULRs across the plant. An important difference between the ULR movement and McDonald's is that the latter's drive is for global expansion while the ULR's drive is a local democratic one. We shall return to this point.

The informant made the point that in the high-tech industry in which he was employed, the most skilled workers were challenged with the reality of such an industry, which constantly demands new skills. This training was provided by the employer and was a requirement on such workers. In contrast, the least skilled were offered very few training opportunities by the company. The consequence of this for the role of

ULRs is that they may be much more useful to lower-skilled and unskilled workers than to the most skilled. He was, however, hesitant about this judgement. He went on to say: 'Even so, ULRs were having demands made on them in ways very similar to that reported by PCS'. Oddly, although the company provided foreign language learning lessons, workers still requested ULRs where and when they might learn a foreign language for their own purposes. When asked about the role of ULRs, he said: 'It's a good idea but it's still new, but it really will develop'.

### McDonald's (Big Macs)

McDonald's expresses a commitment to enabling its employees to move to promoted posts by engaging with workplace and other forms of learning. It sets out with some clarity the potential career track of an employee entering with minimal or no qualifications. Beginning in the restaurant as a lowly member of 'crew', McDonald's sets out a route to an executive position. This information is freely available on the company's own website (McDonald's, 2004) and is set out below:

*Restaurant Crew*
As Restaurant Crew, you will learn the basic skills needed to serve customers.

*Second Assistant Manager*
As a Second Assistant Manager, you'll learn the tools of the Quick Service Restaurant industry and will be involved in training, coaching and motivating 60-100 diverse staff members. Your hands-on training will be supplemented with classroom training.

*First Assistant Manager*
As a First Assistant Manager, you'll assist with all aspects of restaurant operations. You'll supervise recruitment and scheduling of restaurant staff and will be responsible for equipment management. As well, you'll be involved in maintaining, directing and increasing sales and profit levels. Your hands-on training will continue to be supplemented by additional classroom training.

*Restaurant Manager*
As a Restaurant Manager, you'll be fully accountable and responsible for the operation, profitability and management of a multi-million dollar business. You'll establish goals and objectives to maintain and enhance total customer satisfaction and to help build the McDonald's brand in your community.

At this level, you'll receive ongoing business/management
skills training and development.

Ambitious and talented restaurant managers have the opportunity to
extend their career paths into other disciplines related to the McDonald's
business, such as field operations, training, purchasing, human
resources, marketing and more. At the highest level, McDonald's offers
executive development seminars and executive coaching.

The national director for training, learning and development
confirmed that the training on offer can and does lead to promotion to
the highest ranks. He stated that all employees are expected to engage in
training and that the training is progressive and ongoing. In his particular
case, he began his career in McDonald's as restaurant crew and by dint of
following the learning opportunities now occupies a national executive
position. In his experience, this is not unusual and is a common feature
in all the countries in which McDonald's operates. While there may be
some local variation to meet regional, political and cultural differences,
the organisation is seeking to establish a global standard.

As the organisation argues, 'McDonald's strives to provide the best
possible training and career long learning opportunities to achieve our
vision of being recognised as the world's best developer of people'
(McDonald's, 2004). Our informant confirmed that this was the case. He
stated that the career development training was open to all. Where
management might direct equally, individual workers are encouraged to
request further training. The training is directed at organisational
development in the first instance. However, inherent in all the training
opportunities, according to our informant, are aspects of transferable
skills and knowledge – and, frequently, an element of refinement to
reflect the local culture.

### Discussion

It has been a common theme in the developed world that successful
economic development is dependent on the knowledge and skills of the
workforce. The 'upskilling' agenda is common to governments and large
companies. For instance, one of the major focuses of the New Labour
administration in the United Kingdom has been both the development of
new skills and the enhancement of established skills. This agenda is also
a major focus for the Confederation of British Industry (CBI) (CBI, 2003,
2004; CBI & TUC, 2002) and the Institute of Directors (Walsh, 2004;
Wilson, 2004). We discern two different, but related, policies here, the
first to do with enhancing the skills of the existing workforce, and the
second to do with providing skills for the unskilled or low-skilled to
enable them to progress as well as benefiting the organisation. Clearly,
both national governments and private companies share a desire to
develop the skills of the workforce and the potential workforce. In the

private sector, albeit a highly specialised sector, McDonald's has pursued this agenda vigorously and, arguably, more rigorously than the majority of other companies. Significant, for us, is McDonald's desire to provide a training programme which will enable progression from the shop floor to the executive office.

Training is obviously beneficial to the organisation. Much training provided by private companies and state agencies is best described as 'organisational learning', that is, it is primarily for the benefit of the organisation, rather than the individual. Even when training is highly specified it may lead to career enhancement, and this has obvious personal benefits. It is an interesting feature of the McDonald's programme that, alongside its organisational aims, it provides career enhancement for individuals. As our case study shows, opportunities to learn are available to everyone who works in the organisation. We might contrast this with companies which have a less inclusive view of opportunities to learn. The United Kingdom government's somewhat unexpected provision of statutory rights for ULRs is a policy drive towards organisational learning. What we discern from our case studies is that there has been an unexpected outcome from the policy and the legislation. This is acknowledged by the findings in a recent report from the Chartered Institute of Personnel and Development (CIPD) that found ULRs can be 'important allies in promoting the value of learning and training ... are effective in generating "bottom up" demand for learning' and 'have a significant role in engaging workers who might otherwise be reluctant to discuss their learning needs' (CIPD, 2004, p. 10).

We acknowledge that as a global company, McDonald's has done a great deal through its training programme to enhance the careers of some of the most disadvantaged members of developed societies. This must have some personal spin-offs. In contrast, the account we have collected of ULRs indicates a move towards lifelong learning rather than a simple organisational skill agenda. PCS ULRs report that they do not see it as their job to persuade or cajole their members to simply follow the skills training on offer by the organisation. What they have done is open the door to lifelong learning opportunities for groups of workers who in the past have neither identified nor known about those opportunities.

The evidence from all the literature on learning indicates that downward pressure on people to learn is at best marginally successful. For instance, one of our PCS ULRs reports how the downward pressure on workers to learn new computer skills has led them to devise means of avoiding it, while continuing in their job. We would argue, though, that by developing and supporting lifelong learning what will happen is that the workforce will see itself as a learning workforce rather than as a directed workforce. Seeking advice on ballroom dancing or the learning of Spanish, whilst not connected to workplace skills, will develop an attitude such that workers will engage with new learning. If we were really bold, we might argue that because of its democratic and local nature, the creation of ULRs is very important. They are 'agitators' for lifelong learning.

Legislation has now given the ULRs a security not enjoyed by trade unionists in the past eager to offer educational opportunities to fellow members and this could be the most significant educational policy of the 21st century. Linked to this is the enthusiasm for learning in general expressed by the representatives: they have a vision of lifelong learning that goes beyond simply 'upskilling the workforce'. It may be that for the first time trade unions will be able to enable their members to engage with education in the way they have always wanted.

### Acknowledgement

We would like to thank the PCS for facilitating our data collection and for providing us with relevant and important documents, and all the participants who gave up their valuable time to assist us in our research.

## References

Amicus (2004) About Us. Available at: http://www.amicustheunion.org

Bakhtin, M. (1981) Discourse in the Novel, in M. Holquist (Ed.) *The Dialogic Imagination: four essays by M. Bakhtin*, trans. C. Emerson & M. Holquist. Austin: University of Texas Press.

Chartered Institute of Personnel and Development (CIPD) (2004) *Trade Union Learning Representatives: the change agenda*. London: CIPD.

Confederation of British Industry (CBI) (2003) *National Skills Strategy and Delivery Plan: CBI Official Response*. London: CBI.

CBI (2004) *Proposals for Reform of 14-19 Qualifications and the Introduction of a Diploma Framework: CBI official response*. London: CBI.

CBI & Trades Union Congress (TUC) (2002) *Brushing up the Basics*. London: CBI.

Cowen, G., Clements, M. & Cutter, J. (2000) *TUC Union Learning Representatives Survey*. Leeds: York Consulting.

Department for Education and Employment (DfEE) (1998) *The Learning Age – a renaissance for a new Britain*. London: DfEE.

Department for Education and Skills (DfES) (2002) *Union Learning Fund – year 6 prospectus*. London: DfES.

Department for Trade and Industry (DTI) & DfEE (2001) *Opportunity for All in a World of Change*. London: Stationery Office.

Labour Research Department (LRD) (2001) *Learning at Work*. London: LRD.

LRD (2003) Survey Shows it's Early Days for Union Learning Reps, *Bargaining Report*, 235(February), pp. 6-8.

Lee, C. (1998) *Learning from Employee Development Schemes*. Brighton: Institute for Employment Studies.

Maguire, M. & Horrocks, B. (1995) *Employee Development Programmes and Lifelong Learning.* Leicester: Leicester University.

McDonald's (2004) *About McDonald's* and *Being the Best through Hamburger University.* Available at: http://www.media.mcdonalds.com/secured/company/investor/index.html and http://www.media.mcdonalds.com/secured/company/training/

Mortimer, K. (1990) EDAP at Ford: a research note, *Industrial Relations Journal,* 21(4), pp. 309-314.

Moser, C. (1999) *Improving Literacy and Numeracy: a fresh start.* London: Department for Education and Skills.

National Literacy Trust (2003) *Union Learning Fund and the Role of Learning Representatives.* London: National Literacy Trust.

Prime R&D (2000) *Learning Representatives Standards.* London: Trades Union Congress.

Public and Commercial Services Union (PCS) (2002) *Bringing Learning into Work.* London: PCS.

Public and Commercial Services Union (PCS) (2003a) *Local Learning Rep Handbook 2003.* London: PCS.

Public and Commercial Services Union (PCS) (2003b) *PCS Rules.* London: PCS.

Public and Commercial Services Union (PCS) (2004) About PCS. Available at: http://www.pcs.org.uk

PCS Organising and Learning Services (2003) *PCS Learning Representatives: survey of activities.* London: Public and Commercial Services Union.

Rose, A.D., Jeris, L.H. & Smith, R.L. (2004) Adult Educators in Steel Mill Learning Centres: shaping practice through professional development. Paper presented at American Educational Research Association Annual Conference, Enhancing the Visibility and Credibility of Educational Research, San Diego, 12-16 April.

Trades Union Congress (TUC) (2001) *The Smart Set – union learning reps at work.* London: TUC.

Trades Union Congress (TUC) (2002) *The Quiet Revolution – the rise of the union learning representative.* London: TUC.

TUC Learning Services (2004) *Union Learning Really Takes Off.* London: TUC Learning Services. Available at: http://www.learningservices.org.uk

Vincenzi, C. & Fairhurst, J. (2002) *Law and the European Community,* 3rd edn. London: Longman.

Walsh, J. (2004) *Salary Sacrifice and IT Skills: an IOD survey.* London: Institute of Directors.

Wilson, R. (2004) *The Government's Skills Strategy for the Nation: Strengths, Weaknesses and Future Priorities.* London: Institute of Directors.

CHAPTER 8

# Continuing Professional Development and the Health Service in England: the nursing perspective

## YVONNE HILL

### Introduction

The importance of continuing professional development (CPD) in nursing in England has increased since the early 1990s when all pre-registration nursing programmes were brought into the higher education system and raised to a minimum of diploma level under Project 2000. This left most of the existing nurses less well qualified than new entrants to the profession. This resulted in a commitment by the United Kingdom Central Council for Nursing, Midwifery and Health Visiting (UKCC) and the national boards for nursing and midwifery to establish a framework for CPD and introduce mandatory updating for re-registration. Since then, universities and colleges of higher education have developed and expanded their involvement in CPD by providing portfolios of programmes, courses/modules and training to meet individual, organisational and professional needs. The thrust in the early days was to facilitate existing nurses to gain academic awards equivalent to those pursued through the Project 2000 scheme. The current government's agenda for health care (Department of Health (DoH), 1997, 1998) requires that there should be better outcomes for patients and clearer links between pre- and post-registration education. Toon (1997) and Grant & Stanton (1998) advocate that publicly funded CPD should be judged by its impact on health care.

This chapter appraises the political, professional, employer and individual agendas for CPD in Great Britain, proposes models to meet these various needs and demands and examines the evidence of the impact of CPD on patient outcomes.

### Context of CPD in Nursing: policies, drivers and values

CPD has been mandatory in nursing in the United Kingdom since 1998 as part of self-regulation and post-registration education and practice requirements (UKCC, 1995, 1997) and requires nurses to undertake a minimum level of study as a requirement of their tri-annual re-registration. It is an acknowledgement by the profession (UKCC, 2000) that registration at diploma or degree level is not enough to sustain a nurse through a career and maintain competent practice. Coupled with this is the notion of lifelong learning, which the DoH (1998, p. 42) views as an 'investment in quality' defined as:

> a process of lifelong learning for all individuals and teams which meets the needs of patients and delivers the health outcomes and health care priorities of the NHS [National Health Service], and which enables professionals to expand and fulfil their potential.

The concept of lifelong learning first came to prominence in the early 1970s and received endorsement through the Dearing Report (National Committee of Inquiry into Higher Education, 1997) and the Fryer Report (Fryer, 1997), followed by *The Learning Age* (Department for Education and Employment, 1998), in which learning was described as the key to economic growth and affluence. The English National Board for Nursing, Midwifery and Health Visiting (1995) published a document, *Creating Lifelong Learners,* which emphasised the view that nursing required career-long professional education and that, as new and challenging roles emerged, nurses needed to be adequately prepared.

The lifelong learning agenda has had a profound impact on CPD for nurses. Apart from registered practitioners being required to show evidence of updating at their tri-annual re-register, they are expected by their employer to achieve at least diploma status as well as undertaking courses appertaining to their particular professional role (Hemsley-Brown & Humphreys, 1998). It appears that an overriding motivation to participate was employer- rather than employee-led.

Gorard et al (1998) identified five determinants of lifelong learning:

- time – age and past experience of participation;
- place – local opportunities, culture and opportunity;
- gender – women tend to participate in front-loaded provision;
- family – occupational class, educational experience and religion;
- initial schooling – experience of success or failure may influence later learning.

Whilst most of these are fairly obvious micro-determinants, it is not clear how they interact at a macro-level with employer needs and government-led policies. These include modernisation of the NHS (NHS Executive, 1997; DoH, 1998), which has added additional impetus to lifelong learning. It is seen as key to clinical governance and clinical effectiveness. A challenge here is the need to change the culture and set of values in the NHS if continuing improvement is to be made. At the heart of these macro-drivers is improvement in patient care and outcomes, and the nursing strategy document *Making a Difference* (DoH, 1999) is quite clear that CPD is not for a few willing participants, but an essential part of the job. This is reinforced by the *Agenda for Change Proposed Agreement* (DoH, 2003a) and *The NHS Knowledge and Skills Framework and Related Development* (DoH, 2003b). Benton (2003) argues that the *Agenda for Change Proposed Agreement* is more far-reaching than just about pay and is likely to change radically the shape of CPD. Education providers could be pushed towards a competency model rather than knowledge transfer, as many would view it now.

Individual responses to the political and professional drivers have been mixed and are often influenced by negative and positive forces at play in both their personal and professional lives. McGivney (1993) cites Cross's (1981) 'chain of response' model, which starts with the individual and ends with external influences. There are seven interacting links in the chain, and the more positive each stage is moved through, the more likely he or she is to reach the final stage, to participate. The seven stages are:

- learner's own self-evaluation;
- learner's attitude to education;
- motivation to learn;
- life transitions;
- opportunities and barriers;
- information on educational opportunities;
- the decision to participate.

The majority of nurses are women. Research on enrolled nurses participating in conversion courses to first-level nursing registration suggests that life transitions play a big part in women's lives (Hill & MacGregor, 1998). Those who did not seek further study or discontinued appeared unable to cope with the added demands of full- or part-time study. Added to this, the notion of career and personal motives for studying became entangled. An initial response was improvement of career prospects but later this became enmeshed with a desire to overcome powerlessness, marginalisation and fragmentation throughout their lives. Kember (1999) supports the view that successful mature students on part-time courses are those who are able to integrate family, work, study and social demands into their lives. They tend to have an internal locus of control, unlike the students who discontinue or are unsuccessful. He found that a supportive and tolerant family was very important, as the student had to negotiate with family and friends to accommodate the study. Employers and colleagues were also influential in a successful outcome. For successful integration, he argues, there needs to be a renegotiation of social and work positions which may upset other members of the individual's family, colleagues and friends. Dowswell et al (1998a) supported these findings. Roles as parent, spouse and home-carer had to be modified, as well as negotiations with work colleagues, to cover when study time was required.

Benn et al (1998) explore some illuminating insights into women and continuing education which are pertinent to nursing. They take the stance that women undertaking continuing education are collectively a group who have special features in common. In Hill et al's (1997) earlier study on enrolled nurses, group identity and commonality were very important in sustaining effort and focus. In any CPD provision, but particularly in nursing, with its large female workforce, all of the above are likely to have an impact and will, in part, determine success or failure for all concerned.

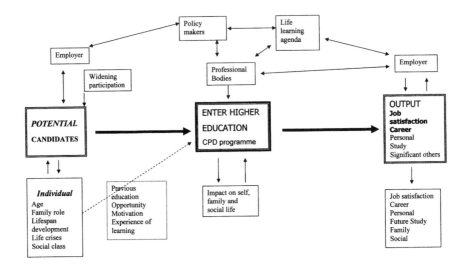

Figure 1. Interacting nature of CPD with various players.

The discussion above forms the starting point for considering CPD for nursing and Figure 1 illustrates the interactive nature of all the dimensions which come into play in nurses' lives, particularly for women, as they make decisions about participation in further study and the likely outcomes.

### Models of CPD

Sadler-Smith et al (2000) argue that there are three main functions of CPD. These are survival, maintenance and mobility, to which a fourth, that of personal achievement, may be added.

Survival fits well with the mandatory requirement by the Code of Professional Conduct (Nursing and Midwifery Council [NMC], 2002) that commits nurses to keep up to date and requires them to undertake a minimum of 35 hours over three years. Failure to do so could result in them being removed from the NMC register. It does just enough to meet the professional requirements but fails to take the practitioner beyond the bare minimum of updating. This fits well with an *instrumental model.* It achieves the mandatory requirement, which is clearly important for the individual and his/her employer. It is focused on ongoing competence; however, it may fail to broaden and improve skills and knowledge to any real extent, with nurses expressing little interest in participation. It is argued that this model is the one that nursing is focused on primarily. As Dowswell et al (1998b) found, nurses expressed resentment at the perceived lack of funding for CPD activities and the lack of time to undertake them. The 'laggards' described by Cervero (1988) would fit this scenario. Mandatory schemes such as the one operating in nursing are at odds with the values and beliefs of lifelong learning in that there is no guarantee of a change in practice or level of competence. It may, as Lawton (2003) suggests, ensure that the 'laggards' participate even if reluctantly.

The maintenance function is the closest fit to lifelong learning in which personal and professional development are paramount. It is systematic, planned and executed in a framework of personal, professional and organisational goals. Competence and benchmarking are also of importance within this model. It best fits an *empowerment model* but could also encompass a *competency model* too. Here a significant factor is individual motivation, which, as suggested by Furze & Pearcey (1999), is one of the most important factors in the outcome of CPD. Earlier writers (Larcombe & Maggs, 1991; Turner, 1991) argued that CPD provided nurses with personal satisfaction as well as greater awareness of professional issues. It has to be said, however, that there is little empirical evidence to support many of these claims, but intuition suggests that it must be 'doing some good' to the individual and profession. Table I identifies key features of the different CPD models.

The mobility function principally aims to increase an individual's employability. Evidence of further study, particularly if it has led to additional awards, is likely to enhance a person's chances of gaining promotion or obtaining a job if changing geographical areas. It has been influential in future development, particularly since nurses are required to keep a personal professional portfolio. The *'top-up' model,* in which diploma-registered nurses undertake further study to gain credit for a higher award, is being pursued by many Project 2000 nurses. This is also the case for many pre-Project 2000 practitioners. They initially top-up to a diploma and some may continue to degree level. Likewise enrolled nurses 'convert' to first-level registration to enhance their employment opportunities and many will continue their studies to gain a diploma and then a degree. A few are continuing on to master's programmes. Within these groups of people, their motivation to study could fit all three functions, survival, maintenance or mobility. From a small study by Hill & MacGregor (1998) it seems many nurses come to study reluctantly or, at the very least, lacking in confidence, but if they are successful, many become highly motivated and progress beyond any aspirations they previously held.

| Model | Functions | Features |
|-------|-----------|----------|
| Instrumental | Survival | On-the-job competencies/skills<br>Meets mandatory updating<br>May improve patient outcomes<br>Extrinsic drivers |
| Empowerment | Maintenance<br>Personal<br>achievement | Lifelong learning, systematic,<br>planned linked to personal,<br>professional and organisational goals<br>May provide liberal education<br>Individual motivation |
| Competency | Maintenance | Linked to employability/promotion<br>Improvement of patient outcomes<br>Extrinsic and intrinsic driver |
| 'Top-up' | Mobility | Employability, promotion<br>Intrinsic driver |
| Training | Skills and related<br>knowledge | On-the-job to meet immediate needs<br>Organisational driver |

Table I. Features of the CPD models.

On the other hand, 'topping-up' can result in a fragmented collection of units of learning which bears little relevance to the context in which the nurse works and lacks coherence. The 'getting through it' to gain the qualification is seen as more important than the professional outcomes. This may be due to lack of involvement of managers, who may fail to encourage or influence choice and direction. It is not clear whether a fragmented curriculum matters to the outcome or prevents individuals transferring the knowledge and skills to their own practice area. On the other hand, it is assumed that good choice and support do result in improved knowledge and skills and professional status, and alongside that, personal growth and increased confidence. The knowledge and skills framework will attempt to link the two together and show evidence of levels of competence before and after study/training intervention.

The final feature, that of personal achievement, is closely aligned to the liberal education movement in which study enhances one's ability to transfer intellectual and other skills to a variety of situations. It is education which goes beyond competencies and learning outcomes and offers a broad vision of the world. Edwards (1993) suggests that many women returned to study not for instrumental reasons but for personal development and interest and it was often dissatisfaction with their work position that led them to undertake further study. The women in Edwards's (1993) study thought higher education was viewed as prestigious and for 'intelligent' people. It conferred a sense of importance and status and lent weight to their views in society and the workplace. The contrasting understandings and experiences of these students formed a base for connections and separations between family and education, causing conflicts and tensions in many instances. Here one sees a thoroughbred model of CPD which is on a higher echelon than organisational and professional goals.

Waterman et al (1995) advocate a career-resilient workforce in which employers give individuals opportunities to develop skills and knowledge to keep pace with changing needs of companies. It requires flexibility in employees, awareness of their own strengths and weaknesses and involvement in company strategy in looking for new opportunities. This, it is argued, requires a broader education than that prescribed by a professional body or NHS trust. How could this type of approach be applied to the NHS? In such a bureaucratic organisation it is difficult to imagine how. A challenging, opposing viewpoint to the one being advocated by government is one in which a broader education may effect change more easily than one driven down a narrow path of competencies.

So it is argued in this section that a number of different models are at play and, for many nurses, no single model is used when deciding to participate in or continue with CPD. There are many factors which interplay, including personal, family and social reasons.

This debate has centred so far around 'education' but there is another dimension, that of 'training'. This is often referred to as a 'quick fix' which has little, if any, underlying theory, no academic credits and no progression towards an award. It enables practitioners to take on new skills, or meet mandatory requirements of their employer such as fire training or moving and handling. It is difficult to view education and training as being compatible but in a practice-based profession it could be argued that there is an element of training in the achievement of competency. There is no doubt, if one views it from a patient perspective, that training to gain competence in a skill is enormously important, but whether it could be classified as CPD is another debate outside the remit of this chapter.

### Challenges

There is a long way to go before there is structured education for registered nurses that is linked to individual, professional and organisational needs. 'Protected learning time' is virtually non-existent in most areas and it is difficult for nurses to access CPD despite enormous improvements in modes of delivery and increased flexibility. Healy (2003) stresses the importance of 'joined-up thinking' particularly as there are two reviews being undertaken at the current time by the NMC and the University of Salford commissioned by the DoH.

A tension exists between knowledge and skills and who should lead any development. Armstrong & Adam (2002) advocate a collaborative model which is NHS-led and working in collaboration with higher education. This ensures that education provision is proactive in meeting the needs of the service. Often, however, provision is led by the education provider, which may result in learning which is either inappropriate or not responding quickly enough to current practice needs. It may, as Jordan (2000) argues, reflect educators' research interests rather than those of practice outcomes. Even if the learning is useful, nurses, highly motivated and wanting to implement change, may find the culture frustrating and a disparity between theory and reality on returning to their clinical area. Armstrong & Adam (2002) found that some students reported having their wings clipped when they tried to implement change and being made to slot back in. Clearly support from managers and colleagues is vital to effect change in practice.

In addition to this, Lawton & Wimpenny (2003) argue that from a review of the literature, there is no real evidence that CPD achieves its goal of maintaining or enhancing standards of competence, if indeed that is what it is trying to achieve. The link to patient outcomes is equally tenuous. However, it is accepted by them and Jordan (2000) that there is a dearth of good-quality research on which to make a sound judgement on this matter.

### Has CPD Been Successful so far?

Presented below are four case studies of nurses who have undertaken CPD in the last seven years. They represent a cross-section of 'typical' nurses working in a locality in the United Kingdom. Their names have been changed.

#### Example 1 – Jenny

Jenny is a single parent with three children, and works full-time in a medical ward. She has no academic qualifications but is accredited with a higher education certificate by virtue of her nursing qualification gained in 1988. Time is precious and she is reluctant to spend time studying, although does the occasional training day providing it is in her work time. Her manager requested her to undertake a Preparation of Mentors course so that she can assess students' practice. After much reluctance, a shaky start and retaking the assignment, Jenny eventually gained 30 level 2 credits and is now able to assess nursing students. After a break of six months, she then signed up for a diabetic care course which she anticipates will be useful for practice. Jenny finds it difficult but does admit to having benefited from studying and recognises an added bonus which she had not anticipated, that of providing a good role model for her children and their school work. For Jenny, survival is crucial and gaining academic credit towards an award is not considered important at this stage.

### Example 2 – Michele

Michele is a diplomate and has been working as a registered nurse for a year in a surgical ward. She is highly motivated and wants to gain a degree as soon as possible. She is less concerned with what constitutes the 'top-up' degree except for the Preparation of Mentors course, which is essential for a higher grade. Michele thinks there is a clear link between academic success and career progression. Her manager thinks she should improve her competency as a staff nurse before embarking on more study.

### Example 3 – Joan

Joan works as a staff nurse in an intensive therapy unit (ITU) and is keen to enable her to enhance her skills in practice. She thinks that competency must play an important part in any CPD and therefore that it is essential for lecturers to be credible in practice. As time is limited, Joan is interested only in undertaking study that is directly related to her field of work, although she does not rule out obtaining a degree through this means at some time in the future. She is hoping to gain 60 credits at level 3 from the ITU course.

### Example 4 – Jim

Jim trained as an enrolled nurse in 1982, and is now a ward manager of a surgical ward. He completed a 'conversion course' to level 1 registration, gaining 60 credits at level 2 and then 'topped-up' to a diploma with four more modules. His career, having stagnated for many years, progressed with promotion to the post of junior ward manager, which he attributes to study and the increased motivation and confidence that it gave him. He is half-way through a degree, which he sees as being important to his position. He is also undertaking an NHS leadership programme, which does not offer academic credits but requires study time.

In three of these cases, competency and skills for the job are central to engagement in study, either organisationally or individually driven. The fourth case is more concerned with career acceleration, although currently there is no explicit link between academic and professional criteria for most nursing jobs in the NHS. Motivation to study will always be varied, as will changing life circumstances, and therefore a flexible and open system is essential to accommodate the needs of everyone, whether they are required or want to undertake further study. There is also a need for managers to take an active interest in staff engagement in CPD to maximise effort in relation to the individual and the organisation.


**Future Trends**

There are three key influences which are likely to impact on future CPD provision.

The first driver is the Agenda for Change (DoH, 2003a), which is based on competence-based pay progression. Career ladders are not unique to the United Kingdom, but have been evolving in the USA and other parts of the world over the past 15 years (Buchan, 1997). Competence is defined by the World Health Organisation as knowledge, skills and behaviours and attitudes. The Agenda for Change addresses the first two but not the third, which might prove to be a problem, as reform often relies on the changing of behaviour and attitudes. Educators must rise to the challenge if the framework is to be successful in all three dimensions. One would assume that the roll-out of the framework will be linked to a robust evaluation to measure its benefits to the organisation, the patient and the student. Benton (2003) foresees that the Agenda for Change has potential far-reaching consequences for job redesign and the nursing profession.

The second dimension is how the rolling-out of a CPD national framework will affect local provision linked to the Agenda for Change. It will depend on how it fits with organisational and managerial goals at local levels. Whilst a national framework has the potential to offer consistency and commonality across boundaries, it also has the potential to be too general and lacking in specificity. With two reviews being undertaken at the current time, there is concern that it may result in contradictory conclusions (Healy, 2003).

The third influence is flexibility and modes of delivery with more concentration on work-based learning and accreditation of prior experiential learning. As protected time and access have been identified as key determinants of successful study, there is a need to offer blended learning which aims to enhance accessibility and variety. Work-based learning enables practice initiatives to be developed and gaps in knowledge and skills to be filled. Clearly appraisal and personal development plans are crucial to this and must be taken seriously.

## Conclusion and Recommendations

Existing research over the last two decades shows little empirical evidence that CPD has significantly enhanced patient care. This may reflect the quality of the research or the difficulties in establishing a link between CPD and patient outcomes. However, there is general agreement in the literature that it is a 'good thing'. The government is continuing to pour resources into it, which suggests there is an attempt to use it as a performance management tool on the one hand and to effect patient outcomes on the other.

CPD in nursing is at a crucial stage of development. With two frameworks, one about competence-related pay and the other to establish a common educational framework, it is not clear how these will impact, but job redesign and competence-linked education are likely to be in that frame as well as a wide range of informal development activity to support progression and competence. It is hoped that the investment in these frameworks will result in lifelong learning as well as improved care and outcomes for the patient/client.

## References

Armstrong, D.J. & Adam, J. (2002) The Impact of a Postgraduate Critical Care Course on Nursing Practice, *Nurse Education in Practice*, 2, pp. 169-175.

Benn, R., Elliott, J. & Whaley, P. (Eds) (1998) *Educating Rita and her Sisters*. Leicester: National Institute of Adult Continuing Education.

Benton, D. (2003) Agenda for Change: job evaluation, *Nursing Standard,* 17(36), pp. 39-42.

Buchan, J. (1997) Climbing the Clinical Ladder, *Nursing Standard*, 12(3), pp. 22-23.

Cervero, R. (1988) *Effective Continuing Education for Professionals.* San Francisco: Jossey-Bass.

Department for Education and Employment (1998) *The Learning Age: a renaissance for new Britain.* Cm 3790. London: HMSO.

Department of Health (DoH) (1997) *The New NHS: modern, dependable.* London: DoH.

Department of Health (DoH) (1998) *A First Class Service: quality in the NHS.* London: DoH.

Department of Health (DoH) (1999) *Making a Difference – strengthening the nursing, midwifery and health visiting contribution to health and health care.* London: DoH.

Department of Health (DoH) (2003a) *Agenda for Change Proposed Agreement.* London: DoH.

Department of Health (DoH) (2003b) *The NHS Knowledge and Skills Framework and Related Development Review.* London: DoH.

Dowswell, T., Hewison, J. & Millar, B. (1998a) Enrolled Nurse Conversion: trapped into training, *Journal of Advanced Nursing,* 28(3), pp. 540-547.

Dowswell, T., Hewison, J. & Millar, B. (1998b) Motivational Forces Affecting Participation in Post-registration Degree Courses and Effects on Home and Work-life. A Qualitative Study, *Journal of Advanced Nursing,* 28(6), pp. 1326-1333.

Edwards, R. (1993) *Mature Women Students.* London: Taylor & Francis.

English National Board for Nursing, Midwifery and Health Visiting (1995) *Creating Lifelong Learners: guidelines for programmes leading to the qualification of specialist practitioner.* London: English National Board for Nursing, Midwifery and Health Visiting.

Fryer, R. (1997) *Learning for the Twenty First Century. First Report of the National Advisory Group for Continuing Education and Lifelong Learning.* Sheffield: National Advisory Group for Continuing Education and Lifelong Learning.

Furze, G. & Pearcey, P. (1999) Continuing Education in Nursing: a review of the literature, *Journal of Advanced Nursing,* 29(2), pp. 355-363.

Gorad, S., Rees, G. & Fevre, R. (1998) Learning Trajectories: travelling towards a learning society, *International Journal of Lifelong Education,* 17(8), pp. 400-410.

Grant, J. & Stanton, F. (1998) *The Effectiveness of Continuing Professional Development,* 2nd edn. London: Joint Centre for Education in Medicine.

Healy, P. (2003) Joined-up Thinking 'Vital' to Separate CPD Reviews, *Nursing Standard,* 18(3), p. 4.

Hemsley-Brown, J. & Humphreys, J. (1998) Opportunity or Obligation? Participation in Adult Vocational Training, *Journal of Vocational Education and Training,* 50(3), pp. 355-373.

Hill, Y. & MacGregor, J. (1998) An EN Conversion Course: does it make a difference? *Journal of Nursing Management,* 6, pp. 173-180.

Hill, Y., MacGregor, J. & Dewar, K. (1997) Access to Higher Education, *Quality Assurance in Education,* 5(2), pp. 73-79.

Jordan, S. (2000) Educational Input and Patient Outcomes: exploring the gap, *Journal of Advanced Nursing,* 31(2), pp. 461-471.

Kember, D. (1999) Integrating Part-time study with Family, Work and Social Obligations, *Studies in Higher Education,* 24(1), pp. 109-124.

Larcombe, K. & Maggs, C. (1991) *Process for Identifying the Continuing Professional Education Needs of Nurses, Midwives and Health Visitors: an evaluation. Report for the English National Board for Nursing, Midwifery and Health Visiting (Project Paper 5).* London: English National Board for Nursing, Midwifery and Health Visiting.

Lawton, S. (2003) Continuing Professional Development: a review, *Nursing Standard*, 17(24), pp. 41-44.

Lawton, S. & Wimpenny, P. (2003) Continuing Professional Development: a review, *Nursing Standard*, 17(24), pp. 41-44/

McGivney, V. (1993) Participation, Non-participation and Access: a review of the literature, in R. Edwards, S. Sieminski & D. Zeldin (Eds) *Adult Learners, Education and Training*. London: Routledge with Open University.

National Committee of Inquiry into Higher Education (1997) *Higher Education in the Learning Society (Dearing Report)*. Norwich: HMSO.

National Health Service (NHS) Executive (1997) *The New NHS – modern and dependable*. London: DoH.

Nursing and Midwifery Council (NMC) (2002) *Code of Professional Conduct*. London: NMC.

Sadler-Smith, E. (2000) Learning Preferences and Cognitive Style: some implications for CPD, *Management Learning*, 8(4), pp. 66-75.

Toon, P. (1997) Educating Doctors, to Improve Patient Care, *British Medical Journal*, 315, p. 326.

Turner, P. (1991) Benefits and Certificates of Continuing Education: an analytical survey, *Journal of Continuing Education in Nursing*, 22(3), pp. 104-108.

United Kingdom Central Council for Nursing, Midwifery and Health Visiting (UKCC) (1995) *PREP & You. Maintaining Your Registration*. London: UKCC.

United Kingdom Central Council for Nursing, Midwifery and Health Visiting (UKCC) (1997) *PREP and You*. London: UKCC.

United Kingdom Central Council for Nursing, Midwifery and Health Visiting (UKCC) (2000) *UKCC and PREP: the practice standard*. London: UKCC.

Waterman, R.H., Waterman, J.A. & Collard, B.A. (1995) Toward a Career-resilient Workforce, in P. Raggatt, R. Edwards & N. Small (Eds) *The Learning Society: challenges and trends,* pp. 207-220. London: Routledge.

CHAPTER 9

---

# Emerging Themes

## ALEX ALEXANDROU, KIT FIELD & HELEN MITCHELL

It is not an easy task, pulling together the strands in order to present a single coherent model of continuing professional development (CPD), drawing on practices from a range of countries and in a range of professions. Inevitably there is a diverse range of approaches, all determined in part by the particular circumstances. However, there are common threads which serve to link one form of provision to another despite these cultural differences. The outcome is not a simple taxonomy, but a multi-dimensional one, enabling a form of analysis and a sharing of ideas and structures. Interestingly each profession has its own forms of jargon, which to a degree overlap, providing CPD with an identity of its own, regardless of the profession to which each form of provision relates.

As a result of this international, cross-professional analysis, labels cannot be applied to different development programmes. However, common characteristics can be identified, illustrating how sets of circumstances are best served by types of CPD. This level of complexity means that the analysis can show that types of provision 'lean' one way or another. The descriptions of types of CPD represent therefore the extremes to which the types 'lean' rather than a precise set of definitions.

It is worth reminding the reader of the range of professions and forms of development accounted for in this text. The education profession is covered in many forms and across countries. Health professional development is accounted for through an English perspective. Union learning representatives' involvement in professional development is informed by Canadian and US practices. Approaches such as mentoring are accounted for, and the generic themes are applicable across professions.

The range and scope can of course be seen from the chapter headings.

What is not so obvious from a superficial reading are the key similarities and differences, and indeed how a conceptual framework is emerging.

### An Emerging Conceptual Framework

Much is owed to Bolam (1986) for the development of a conceptual framework. Bolam (1986) identified a continuum of CPD provision, ranging from individual-led provision to system-led provision. With the two types at each end of a continuum, and indeed mention of a pendulum swing between the two, Bolam (1986) presents a paradigm consisting of competing elements (Figure 1).

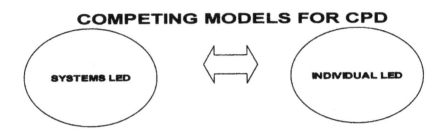

Figure 1. Competing models for CPD.

By system-led Bolam (1986) means a set of training courses designed and supported in order to implement a broader policy. Indeed those who fund the CPD are also the authors of the overarching policy. CPD therefore supports the system, and is part of a managerialist approach to public service leadership. Individual-led CPD is, on the other hand, far more democratic, allowing practitioners themselves to decide on, design and participate in programmes of their own choice, partly for the joy of learning. Both systems have their advantages, although the suggestion is that the two cannot run side by side. As approaches at national, or at least service, level, the two are mutually exclusive.

An analysis of the chapters in this book suggest a third dimension – a profession-led approach. This approach is more about developing the profession from within; its capacity to change, and to develop a sense of professional responsibility in place of accountability. This 'system' has in common with an individual-led approach a devolvement of power from the employer. It has in common with the system-led approach a sense of collective responsibility to a governing body – but in this case to the profession itself in a newly regulated form, rather than the employer. The introduction of a 'middle way', which can lean towards the existing extreme forms in a way that addresses immediate needs, begins to form a complementary model as opposed to the competing models identified in the past. As a single framework it enables analysis of policy and practice in a way that does not exclude forms of CPD which may be necessary in certain circumstances.

This discussion draws on the chapters in this book to illustrate both the advantages and the disadvantages of CPD systems. In each case we wanted to do three things:

1. define the models and relate to real examples presented in this text;
2. present what is good about each model;
3. present what is bad if too much emphasis is placed on each paradigm.


*System-led CPD*

System-led CPD is a system which encourages or requires professionals to participate in learning and development activities with the primary purpose of improving/updating the system. It is therefore top-down, and aims at consistency and coherence. It offers no sense of individual independence or collective autonomy to the profession. Within the health profession the decision to make nursing a graduate profession meant that new nurses were more qualified than experienced nurses. CPD became the means of bridging the gap. The same has happened in the Italian education service – graduate and teacher-trained teachers now enter the profession, and work alongside 'tenured teachers' who may have drifted into the position they find themselves in with no formal training. For Portuguese teachers, escaping a fascist regime, it is no surprise that a system-led process has developed as the speediest way of creating and operating within a new professional culture.

The element of consistency has been achieved often by introducing standards and competencies, along with a career ladder or promotion route which requires the demonstration of the published standards.

Key processes of such a system-led approach are best exemplified in the account given of union learning representatives. The process comprises the establishment of an audit against clear professional standards; tailored provision designed to address perceived areas of professional life in need of development; and career recognition through formal acknowledgement and certification of the fulfilment of higher-level professional standards.

Nurses and teachers find themselves setting targets which relate to national standards associated with a rank or professional position, and Italian teachers and leaders strive to use learning experiences to demonstrate a level of capability. In Scotland successful professional learning is no longer a right, but a responsibility. Teachers and nurses are remunerated according to the level of competence displayed – competence-related pay. Professional status and/or title is attached to a set of imposed standards.

Several indicators demonstrate success in the development of a system-led approach.

Levels of participation by professionals have increased immeasurably as money and rank are attached to the fulfilment of standards. Accountability procedures which involve punitive measures have ensured that professionals are required to keep up to date.

An ageing professional population replaced by younger entrants to the profession who are at least as well, or more, qualified demands that experienced professionals engage in a form of 'catch-up'. Promotion opportunities appear more accessible to 'new professionals' who are more able to demonstrate 'new standards'. This creates a demand for CPD. The Italian experience and that of nurses in the UK serve as good examples.

From the employer's perspective, such a system supports modernisation and the adoption of new practices, with the ultimate aim of wealth creation. A system-led approach to CPD is of benefit during a period of change and leads to a better-qualified, more up-to-date workforce.

There are of course disadvantages. Linking CPD strategies to standards and conditions of service breeds a compliant professional body. As restricted professionals, employees learn to do what they are told very well. System-led CPD does not serve to build a capacity for ongoing change in a dynamic world. Professionals in such a system are not encouraged to challenge or critique current orthodoxies.

Within system-led CPD motivation is extrinsic not intrinsic. Rewards are given for compliance through performance and competence-related pay. A sense of commitment and ownership is not fostered and therefore intrinsic motivation may diminish. System-led CPD leads to changing practice, but not shaping practice.

Funding for system-led CPD is linked to political priorities not perceived professional and practitioner needs. Upskilling to keep pace with change caters only for those who already have the capacity. It does not motivate or cater for the personal needs of the underskilled. Deeper social and professional divisions can emerge. The Portuguese experience shows how science and technology subjects have been favoured.

The profession has no mandate – compliance and conformity are the order of the day. This reduces a capacity to respond to the unexpected and runs the risk of demotivating professionals. It is interesting to note the sudden dip in applications in Scotland for Chartered Teacher status after the initial rush.

*Individual-led CPD*

Individual-led CPD is the provision of learning activities which promote individual learning, which may be unrelated to professional roles. By definition it allows for individual learning styles and preferences, and is built on the principles of lifelong learning and liberal education.

Integrated learning is fostered respecting the learning which takes place through taking part in work and associated social activities. Higher education institutions have provided accreditation which is for the individual, and for teachers and nurses it often involves the negotiation of assessment tasks to enable in-depth study of matters of personal professional interest. For union learning representatives it has involved developing learning opportunities to meet individual wants as opposed to needs. Crucial is the concept of 'paid time off' in order to learn.

Funding may be on an individual basis, which, it seems, reinforces a sense of personal responsibility and a simultaneous respect for the employer, who is seen to take an active interest in the employee's personal development.

Meeting individual wants is personally rewarding, and engenders a sense of being valued. Provision becomes value-driven in that the focus is on the individual rather than corporate outputs. Academic accreditation leads to personal recognition, and the duty of care an external body has relieves any sense of professional manipulation.

Interestingly, too, the account of union learning representative experiences also indicates that learning by choice in a way that meets particular learning preferences assists in the development of a learning organisation. Teachers in Italy and England demonstrate a desire to capture, narrate and make sense of professional experiences. This in turn leads to a sense of empowerment. Personal motivation is enhanced within a climate of individual-led CPD.

Individual-led CPD seems also to improve employer-employee relations. This, coupled with the view that an increased motivation to learn within a culture of learning leads to a more aspirational workforce, points to the positive side of individual-led CPD.

Chapters in this book also point to negative consequences. Previous forms of CPD in Scotland, which could be characterised as individual-led CPD, resulted in an overall sense of spasmodic and disconnected experiences over a period of time. The paradigm lacks accountability, in that the goal, and therefore success, is dependent upon personal satisfaction rather than increased or improved productivity.

Successful engagement is dependent upon 'paid time off'. The provision is also dependent upon an 'agitator' with a mandate from the profession to act on their behalf and access resources from the employer. Inevitably real success and the subsequent institutional development are dependent upon individual enterprise. Equality of opportunity and equity are almost impossible to assure. It is intriguing to note, however, how European funds are being made available to support professional development of this type. The extent to which success can be assured through a regulated system which impacts many different cultures will be interesting to monitor.

### Profession-led CPD

Profession-led CPD is a form of provision designed by and for the profession itself, under the mandate provided by the appropriate government agency.

It is concerned with establishing and maintaining the status and reputation of the profession, and for the benefit of the profession aims to shape rather than respond to changes in practice.

Italian teachers are encouraged to research, develop and experiment, and to develop a bank of professional knowledge through the sharing and dissemination of professional biographies. This form of evidence-based practice respecting the sharing of ideas and the dissemination of qualitative evidence is a means of providing professionals with respect and professional esteem.

Profession-led CPD does not rely on individual whims and aspirations. The 35 hours of compulsory CPD in Scotland places teachers on a par with accountants and the law profession in terms of their responsibility to keep up to date and to develop as professionals. Nurses in England must engage in CPD in order to re-register every three years. This inevitably provides an incentive.

The nursing profession is predominantly female. Women, we are told, work well in collaboration. Profession-led CPD encourages and supports networking as a form of CPD. Given the gender imbalance within public services in favour of women, this new approach seems more appropriate.

The individual professional is provided with a sense of collective responsibility. The exact nature of the training and development undertaken remains, to an extent, the responsibility of the individual. Only the profession itself can recognise the need for a balance between specificity and generalisations. The higher education dominance of accredited CPD in Portugal and indeed elsewhere resonates with the need for the individual to give his/her own CPD a direction and purpose – for which she/he is accountable.

Titles and awards from the profession themselves engender a sense of affiliation and pride in achievement. These, in turn, contribute to a status and profile, tackling the issues associated with recruitment and retention.

Through profession-led CPD the concepts of collaboration and collectivity reduce the notion of 'private practice' previously associated with teaching in England.

The model relies on a professional's sense of responsibility, and therefore it can be argued that the lack of accountability can lead to institutional stagnation. Funding must be from sources other than the employer to reduce vested interests. There is a risk that the individual can pursue personal interests to the detriment of employers and even peers. If the individual's loyalty is exclusively to the professional body she/he is a part of, there is a risk that professional affiliation can lead to a sense of exclusivity and untouchability. Public accountability within public services is essential.

### Recommendations

CPD must not be seen as a means to a particular end but a way of drawing together into a single model what is good within each of the competing models. There are signs across professions and in a range of countries that a complementary model is emerging. This builds upon the strengths of each approach and the goal is to eliminate the risks and weaknesses of each.

## COMPLEMENTARY MODELS FOR CPD

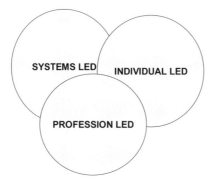

Figure 2. Complementary models for CPD.

Each model should be loosely linked so that it is flexible and able to respond to the particular needs of individuals and groups. Learning and development should motivate individuals through a sense of achievement. The profession and the place of work should acknowledge and recognise successes, and themselves respond positively to what is being and has been learnt. The culture of a learning organisation applies to both the profession and the workplace.

If the two are responsible for and responsive to learning, then the individual will feel empowered and achieve a sense of agency. Shaping practice is about sharing and disseminating; professional pride is built upon a knowledge that there is a knowledge and evidence base which can inform and justify professional action.

Emerging from public service professionals across Europe at this stage is a need to develop and unleash the potential of the workforce by providing learning and development opportunities within a framework which is purposeful and accountable, which motivates and inspires individuals and which engenders a sense of pride and affiliation.

### Reference

Bolam, R. (1986) Conceptually In-service, in D. Hopkins (Ed.) *In-service Training and Educational Development: an institutional survey*. London: Croom Helm.

# Notes on Contributors

**Alex Alexandrou** is a freelance academic and researcher and chair of the International Professional Development Association. His main areas of activity include advising and writing on developments in continuing professional development in the public sector, acting as a course assessor for United Nations-sponsored educational courses and teaching on various national and international MBA courses. Alex also sits on the editorial board of the *Journal of In-service Education*.

**Francesca Brotto** is an experienced teacher, teacher leader, teacher trainer and international projects developer now seconded as advisor and assistant to the director general of the International Relations Department of the Italian Ministry of Education and Research. Her main fields of interest and research are related to the dissemination of good practices and project methodology, to school self-evaluation and new leadership roles, to language teaching and learning and to the European dimension of education.

**Fiona Christie** is a lecturer in Teaching of English to Speakers of Other Languages at the Moray House School of Education in the University of Edinburgh and is mainly involved in the professional development of international teachers of English as a foreign language. She was coordinator of a Scottish Higher Education Funding Council-funded project, based in the Moray House School of Education, to develop and run continuing professional development courses for student teacher mentors. She subsequently worked as a researcher in the Centre for Educational Leadership.

**John Dwyfor Davies** is Professor of Education at the University of the West of England, Bristol, where he was previously a principal lecturer and head of school (Professional and Learning Studies). He has researched and published widely on the themes of inclusive education and professional development.

**Kit Field** is the head of the Department of Professional Development at Canterbury Christ Church University. He is a committee member of the International Professional Development Association and chair of the Universities Council for the Education of Teachers (Continuing

Professional Development) committee. Kit's background is modern foreign languages, and in recent years Kit's research has focused on subject leadership and middle management as well as professional learning.

**Irene Figueiredo** is vice-president of the Polytechnic Institute of Porto and is also a professor of educational policy administration in the School of Education at the Institute, where she is responsible for educational policy studies, school administration and comparative education in initial, continuous and specialised training of teachers, principals and other educators. Irene is a member of several working groups and committees dealing with educational policy and has authored several reports that have been considered at national level by the Portuguese educational authorities.

**Yvonne Hill** is head of adult nursing studies at Canterbury Christ Church University. She has been involved in the continuing professional development (CPD) of nurses and midwives for over 12 years and is actively involved in developing and managing a large portfolio of programmes, courses and study days to service the needs of health care providers and practitioners in Kent. Her research interests include exploring the impact of CPD on both the personal and professional lives of individuals and how prior experiential learning can be used and valued within a CPD framework.

**John Lee** is reader in education in the Faculty of Education, University of the West of England. Recent research includes the education of boys and girls in primary schools, secondary school students and non-attendance at school. He is currently engaged in research into aspects of police training.

**Helen Mitchell** is coordinator for continuing professional development at the University of East London. She has extensive experience in mentoring and mentor education and in pre-service and in-service teacher education as a former postgraduate certificate in education (PGCE) subject leader in the areas of primary science and music. Helen currently leads the mentor training programmes for a primary PGCE course and works in partnership with training schools to develop and deliver mentor training for a range of other courses. She is also a member of the London providers mentor group and has contributed to the development of the London providers mentor training framework. Helen coordinates and teaches on an MA in education practice programme and tutors for an MA by independent study. Helen is also the vice-chair of the International Professional Development Association, and edits the International Professional Development Association newsletter.

**Jim O'Brien** is vice-dean of the Moray House School of Education in the University of Edinburgh and currently director, Centre for Educational Leadership. He has contributed to several national development projects in Scotland including appraisal and review, the Scottish Qualification for Headship and most recently the development of the Standard for Chartered Teacher and associated pilot programmes. At present he is the president of the International Professional Development Association. He has published in the fields of continuing professional development, teacher induction, leadership and management and school improvement.

**Magnus Persson** was a head teacher/school manager for 12 years. At present he is working as the international education manager at the Directorate of Education, Karlstads kommun, Sweden, responsible for local and international educational projects. For eight years he has been coordinating several European projects within the Socrates programme, where he has wide management experience from Comenius 1, 2 and 3 projects as well as extensive practice in international networking. Furthermore, he has been course manager of several European in-service training courses, located in different countries. Since 2003 he has been the coordinator of the European Educational Comenius 3 network 'The Learning Teacher Network'.